Plate I

Harvesting scene outside the walls of Jericho, about 7,000 B.C. The men use antler or wooden sickles with flint blades for reaping the wheat (einkorn). Women are on their way to assist in the harvesting (in some primitive agricultural societies of the present time the reaping is done by women—but see also Fig. 10). The goats are semi-domesticated; the field is irrigated by ditch from a spring. *Drawing by Maurice Wilson.*

British Museum (Natural History)

THE NEOLITHIC REVOLUTION

by Sonia Cole

FIFTH EDITION

Trustees of the British Museum (Natural History)

London: 1970

Price: Five Shillings (25p)

First Edition	1959
Second Edition	1961
Third Edition	1963
Fourth Edition	1967
Fifth Edition	1970

PRINTED IN ENGLAND BY STAPLES PRINTERS LIMITED
AT THEIR KETTERING NORTHANTS ESTABLISHMENT

Contents

Preface to Fifth Edition

The series of exhibits on the evolutionary history of Man in the bays on the west side of the Central Hall include a display in the fourth bay to illustrate the biologically important change in human economy from hunting to farming which began early in post-glacial times, and which has been named the Neolithic Revolution. It was possibly during the Neolithic stage of culture that the main dispersal of the modern races of *Homo sapiens* occurred.

Materials for this Neolithic exhibit were provided by the Departments of Palaeontology, Zoology and Botany, by the Department of British Antiquities of the British Museum at Bloomsbury and, most generously, by a number of other museums including the National Museum, Copenhagen; the Oriental Institute, Chicago; the London University Institute of Archaeology; the Department of Egyptology, University College, London; the Avebury Museum; and the Worthing Museum.

This short handbook was issued to cover the subject in its broader aspects. It was written by Mrs. Sonia Cole, who prepared the exhibit under the general direction of Dr. K. P. Oakley and with the assistance of staff of the Exhibition Section. In the preparation of the sections on the cultivation of plants and the domestication of animals, much helpful advice was received from Dr. W. T. Stearn and the late Professor F. E. Zeuner.

Since the first edition in 1959, progress of research into the origins of Neolithic economy has been so rapid that it has been necessary to print new editions every two years to keep up to date with discoveries. From 1961 onwards, excavations at Çatal Hüyük in Turkey have thrown new light on Neolithic religious beliefs and much else. Other recent excavations, mentioned for the first time in the fourth edition, include among others those at Ali Kosh in Iran and at Nea Nikomedeia in Greece. In this fifth edition, new material has been described from Lepenski Vir in Jugoslavia; and more emphasis has been placed on the way of life of pre-Neolithic peoples, for instance the importance of the harvesting of wild cereals. In general, the text has been expanded con-

v

siderably since the last edition and new distribution maps have been prepared for Fig. 3. Radiocarbon dates have shown that animals were domesticated much earlier than was suspected at the time when this book was written and many new finds are mentioned.

Thanks are due to various authors and institutions for permission to reproduce photographs and figures in the handbook and acknowledgment to them is made in the legends.

January, 1970

H. W. BALL
Keeper of Palaeontology.

I

Introduction

For over a million years, during the Palaeolithic and Mesolithic stages of culture, men lived by hunting and collecting wild plants. This food-gathering economy was gradually supplemented and eventually replaced by one of food production in the Neolithic stage, beginning at least by the eighth millennium B.C. in south-western Asia. The centre for this 'revolution' lay between 30°N and 40°N, stretching for over a thousand miles from western Iran to Greece, including parts of Iraq, Syria, Lebanon, Jordan, Israel and the Anatolian plateau in Turkey. In this area, wheat and barley grew wild, which led to the beginnings of agriculture; here too lived the wild ancestors of goats and sheep, which were probably first domesticated in the Middle East. Wild cattle and pigs had a much wider distribution and were domesticated later, probably from several independent centres.

The change from hunting to farming laid the foundations of civilization. Hitherto, communities had been restricted by the number of game animals and the amount of edible plants available; now it was possible to plant more seed, till more land and breed more animals as the population increased. Many families joined together to help in the communal production of food, as well as in defence against enemies. This sedentary and more economic way of life gave some measure of security and encouraged the arts of civilization. Enough surplus food could be accumulated to support specialized craftsmen, devoting most of their time to the manufacture of tools, pottery, clothing and buildings.

People practised different forms of Neolithic economy, leading to considerable diversification. Interbreeding between indigenous hunters and nomadic pastoralists, for instance, must have given rise to new genetic combinations. Grain farmers, who must exercise skill and foresight, created peasant communities on which the great civilizations of the world were based; root farmers of the tropics, on the other hand, would not have had to expend much effort since Nature did their work for them.

Different altitudes, producing contrasting environments within a limited area, must have provided a strong stimulus to the exchange of products and ideas. Pioneer farming societies, in fact, flourished in such settings: in the Jordan Rift, on the foothills of the Zagros mountains, and later in Meso-America and on the slopes of the Andes. In the first area there were settled villages long before cultivation or domestication took place; then came the 'aceramic' Neolithic—without pottery—with cultivated wheat and barley and domesticated goats. After that, between about 6,000 and 5,000 B.C., there is an archaeological hiatus in this area, a 'lost millennium' which may have been a period of proto-husbandry practised by nomadic populations who would leave few traces. Then came the pottery Neolithic, with dependence on agriculture and selective breeding.

The new way of life began in the well-watered uplands fringing the desert, particularly on the foothills of the Zagros mountains and on the Anatolian plateau. It was not until about 5,500 B.C., some two thousand years later, that farmers moved down to the alluvial plains, irrigated by rivers such as the Tigris and Euphrates. Permanent settlements also grew up at oases such as Jericho, watered by a perennial spring and perhaps aided by attempts at artificial irrigation. In less favoured parts of the world, people practising a shifting hoe-cultivation moved on as soon as the land became exhausted or infested with weeds beyond control; this was the case, for instance, with the earliest European farmers, known as the Danubians, who gradually spread westwards over the lightly forested loess[1] lands of central Europe.

The Neolithic, although often referred to as a period for the sake of convenience, was not confined to a particular period of time, but its duration varied in different areas. In some cases people continued to depend on hunting, fishing and gathering while their more progressive neighbours practised a Neolithic economy. Similarly, Neolithic peoples in certain areas continued to use stone tools long after others were making tools and weapons of bronze or iron. The word 'Neolithic', in fact, simply implies food production based on crops and domesticated stock, without metals.

---

[1] *Loess* is a powdery wind-blown deposit which thickly blanketed extensive areas of Europe beyond the ice sheets during the Glacial period; weathering to a light loam, it forms a very fertile soil, easily worked after being cleared of trees.

The carbon-14 or radiocarbon method of dating has been applied to many Neolithic sites and a firm chronology has now emerged. Consistent results show that in some areas a proto-Neolithic stage with at least semi-permanent settlements began before 8,000 B.C.; a 'pre-pottery' or aceramic Neolithic existed in the Middle East soon after 7,000 B.C.; and a Neolithic with pottery appeared in southern Anatolia before 6,500 B.C.

Results from Zawi Chemi Shanidar village site in northern Iraq suggest that a proto-Neolithic with domesticated sheep began as long ago as 8,900 B.C. This date is some six hundred years before the ending of glacial conditions in northern Europe and the beginning of Mesolithic cultures there. At Jericho, there were proto-Neolithic people about 7,800 B.C. and a pre-pottery or aceramic Neolithic a thousand years later. Other sites with an aceramic Neolithic between 7,000 and 6,000 B.C. include Qalat Jarmo (Iraq) and Ali Kosh (Iran). Ali Kosh, in the Deh Luran valley, is exceptional in that it lies in the now barren alluvial plain of Khuzistan in western Iran outside the present habitat of wild wheat and barley, and at first the economy was based on domesticated goats and sheep, seed collecting and the gathering of a great variety of wild foods, with a strong emphasis also on hunting; grain cultivation appeared somewhat later.

The earliest known Neolithic with pottery appears ar Çatal Hüyük in Anatolia about 6,800 B.C. and at Tepe Guran in Iran about 6,500 B.C. Anatolia was the gateway to Europe and by 5,600 B.C. a pottery Neolithic existed at Nea Nikomedeia in Greek Macedonia. From its nucleus in the Middle East, the new way of life gradually spread along the shores of the Mediterranean and up the valley of the Danube. Radiocarbon dates determined recently suggest that the Neolithic in western Europe began much earlier than had been supposed; the earliest date obtained is about 4,175 B.C. for a Neolithic site in the Netherlands. In Britain, it seems that the Windmill Hill people had arrived before 3,000 B.C., a thousand years earlier than was suggested only a few years ago

The materials illustrating Neolithic culture, particularly in its biological aspects which are our main concern here, have been drawn mainly from sites where conditions of preservation were exceptionally good. For instance at Jarmo, cereal grains and other plant foodstuffs have been carbonized or have left identifiable impressions in the baked clay floors of ovens. Much perishable Neolithic material has been preserved in carbonized form at Çatal Hüyük (*c.* 6,500 B.C.); also in the dry lake beds of the Fayum in Egypt (*c.* 4,500 B.C.) and in the wet lake beds of Switzerland (3,000–2,000 B.C.). Often, too, organic material is well preserved in peat, for instance two Neolithic long-bows of yew found near Glastonbury in Somerset in 1961 which have been dated to about 2,600 B.C.

Although there is no doubt that the Neolithic was a 'revolution' in man's way of life, it has been suggested that the word 'evolution' is more appropriate since the transformation was so gradual. Recent research has shown that there were semi-settled communities, from about 8,900 B.C. onwards, among peoples formerly known as Mesolithic but now generally referred to as proto-Neolithic. The development of full food production was an evolution rather than a sudden revolution; yet there is no doubt that the consequences of this change were revolutionary in the fullest sense of the word.

Time and space relationships of NEOLITHIC and other early cultures in Europe and the Middle East.

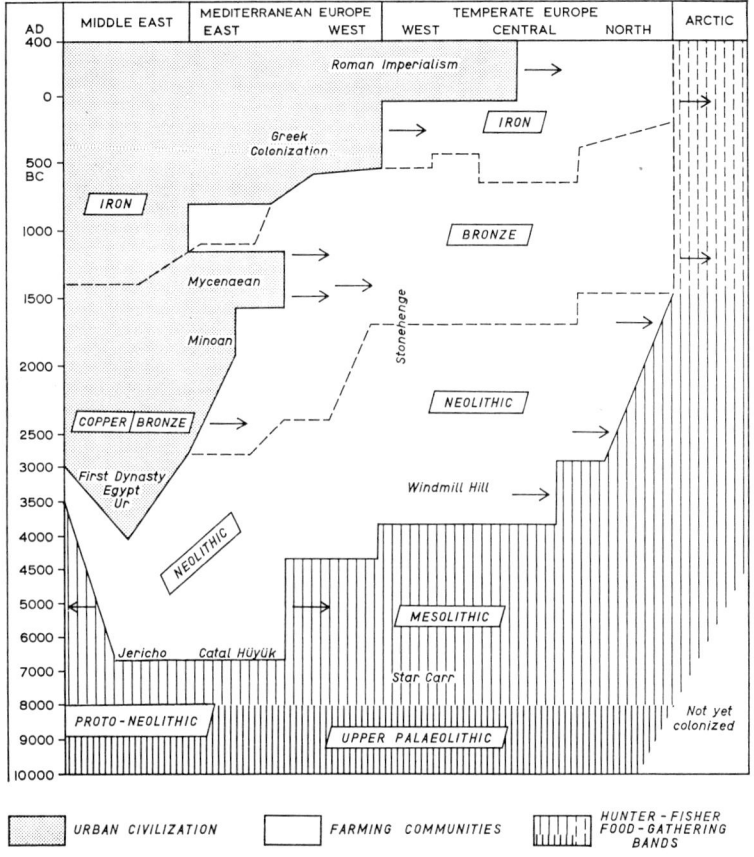

Based on J. G. D. Clark, 1952, with modifications.

Continuance of Hunting and Fishing

Long before cultivation and domestication, there is evidence that man exploited many food resources other than meat obtained by hunting and vegetable foods: birds, for instance, as well as snails, crabs and fish. Evidence from various parts of the world, particularly Jordan and Israel, Yugoslavia and the Sudan, suggests that many of the first people to live in permanent—or at least semi-permanent—settlements were fishermen. At the Lower Natufian site of Eynan on Lake Huleh in Israel, for instance, the inhabitants lived in round stone houses, reaped wild cereals, but depended mainly on fishing. At the remarkable settlement of Lepenski Vir, near the Iron Gates of the Danube in Yugoslavia, pre-Neolithic people were well fed on sturgeon, as well as wild cattle, deer and boars from the forest.

An abundance of game would also have induced hunters to settle in one place, at least seasonally. Examples are Bouqras on the Euphrates, Zawi Chemi Shanidar, and Ali Kosh, where gazelles, onagers and other game were plentiful. During the earliest phase at Ali Kosh (before 6,000 B.C.) hunting accounted for only 25% of the plentiful animal bones, but these made up more than 60% of the total weight of meat; the rest was mainly of domesticated goats and sheep. Hunting, moreover, was just as important when the site was abandoned around 5,600 B.C. as it had been earlier.

It is hardly surprising that hunting and fishing continued to flourish during Neolithic times. Primitive agriculture was certainly a precarious business; harvests must have been unpredictable, sometimes yielding surpluses, more often perhaps with lean years owing to erratic rainfall. The keeping of domestic animals might have been more certain than agriculture, though their feeding at certain times of the year would also have presented problems.

Judging by the equipment found at early settlements, there were groups who, although qualifying as Neolithic because they grew crops and kept domestic animals, in fact lived much as their ancestors had done. Wild animals were important not only as a source of food but also because their hides and bones provided raw materials for making clothing and tools. In Europe the red deer was hunted extensively and a great variety of equipment was made from its hide and antlers.

Interesting evidence of the continued importance of hunting in early Neolithic times, and of the methods of butchering the animals, has been collected recently at Ali Kosh and also at Beidha, near Petra in Jordan. At Ali Kosh, stone meat-choppers and slicing slabs were found and the meat was evidently cooked in brick-lined roasting pits. At the aceramic village of Beidha, a 'butcher's shop' contained articulated joints and horned heads, while another room was full of heavy stone choppers, hammers and grinders. In yet another room, evidently the workshop of a maker of bone tools, a huge pair of ibex horns was found, together with the frontals from which the horns had been cut off.

Animals were hunted in Neolithic times mainly by traps, bow-and-arrow or sling—methods which showed little advance upon those used during the Palaeolithic. Dogs had already been tamed in Northern Europe in Mesolithic times (see p. 22), and very possibly helped man in hunting.

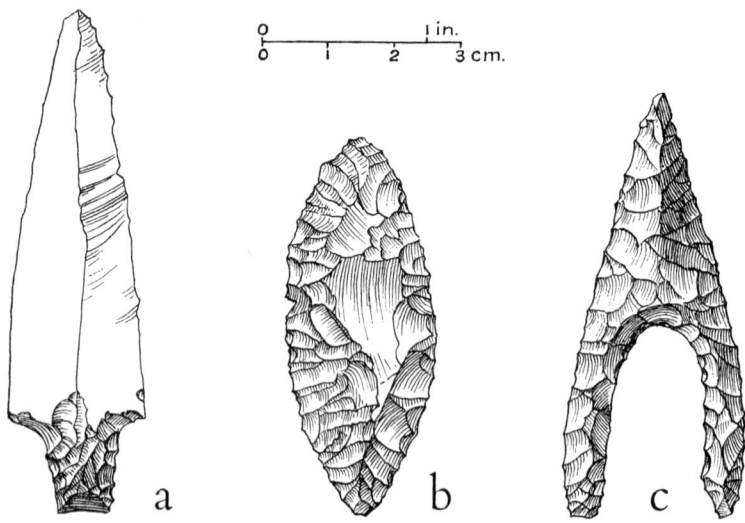

FIG. I. Neolithic flint arrowheads: (a) tanged, Jericho; (b) leaf-shaped, Windmill Hill, Wiltshire; (c) hollow-based, Fayum, Egypt.

Types of arrowhead varied from region to region. Tanged arrow-heads have been found in pre-pottery levels at Jericho and are common at Neolithic sites in the Middle East (Fig. 1*a*). Hollow-based arrow-heads were perfected in Egypt, particularly at the Fayum (Fig. 1*c*). Leaf-shaped arrowheads are characteristic of the earliest Neolithic culture of Britain, that of Windmill Hill (Fig. 1*b*). Sling-stones seem to have been preferred to arrows at many Neolithic sites in western Asia, for instance at Hassuna, Sialk and Ubaid.

Fishing was done by means of hooks, harpoons, nets and traps. Hooks and harpoons were usually made of bone, but at Shaheinab, in the Sudan, shell of the Nile oyster was used for hooks; a series of partly finished specimens shows the stages in their manufacture (Fig. 2, *above*). All early fish-hooks were without barbs. Harpoons had notches or holes for the attachment of the line (Fig. 2, *below*). Fish-traps dating from the Stone Age in Denmark are very similar to modern osier weels used for catching salmon.

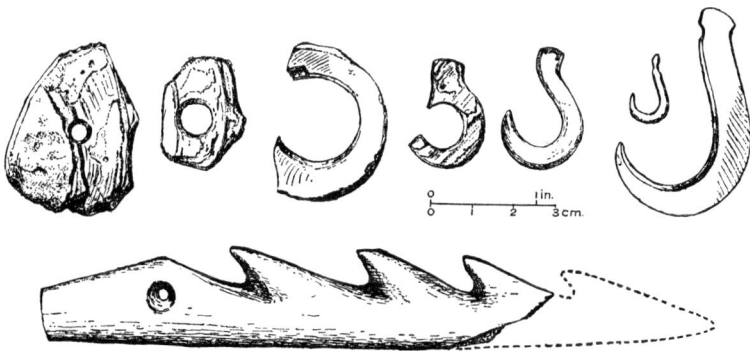

Fig. 2. Above: stages in the manufacture of fish-hooks made from the shell of the Nile oyster. Below: bone harpoon with hole for the attachment of the line. Neolithic; Shaheinab, Sudan. *Based on A. J. Arkell.*

Origins of Plant Cultivation

Every food plant of major importance to mankind was grown in the Neolithic stage of culture, just as all the main animals reared for meat today were domesticated during the Neolithic. Plant cultivation may have started before stock keeping, though there is evidence that mixed farming was practised very early in the Neolithic. Possibly agriculture was at first mainly the concern of women, whereas animals were domesticated by the men, whose traditional occupation had always been hunting while the women gathered vegetable foods.

In early times various forms of agriculture were no doubt practised in different parts of the world just as they are today, but it is almost impossible to find evidence of, for instance, the cultivation of tropical root crops. With grain we are on surer ground, since the carbonized remains or impressions are sometimes preserved.

Very likely grain cultivation started accidentally. Wild cereals would have been collected from afar and brought to the settlement, where seeds would have been dropped and the inhabitants would in due course harvest the crop which miraculously appeared on their doorstep. The purposeful sowing of seeds would have come later, as cause and effect became apparent.

The advantages of cultivating plants were probably first realized by groups of food-gatherers, such as the proto-Neolithic Natufians, living a fairly static existence on the grassy uplands bordering the arid plains of the Middle East. In this area (Fig. 3), the annual grasses included wild forms of wheat and barley, which are tolerant of low rainfall and yield large enough grains in sufficient quantity to encourage harvesting.

Experiments carried out in Turkey by J. R. Harlan showed that the harvesting of wild cereals could have made a significant contribution to the diet of pre-Neolithic peoples. Using a flint-bladed sickle, he gathered enough wild wheat in an hour to produce 1 kilo of grain—which, incidentally, proved to be almost twice as rich in protein as cultivated wheat. A family working for three weeks when the wild wheat is ripe, he suggests, could gather more grain than they could

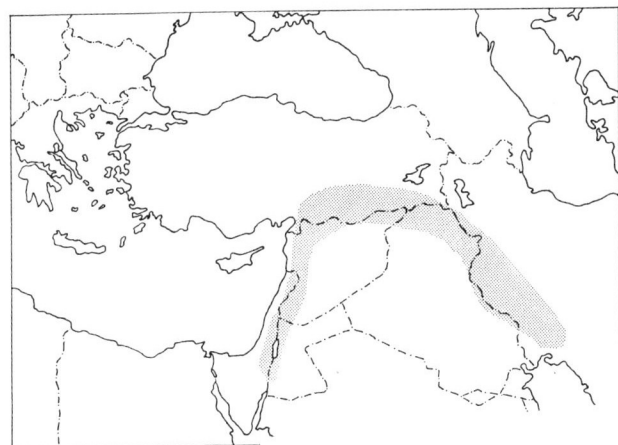

Fig. 3a. The distribution of wild w
After H

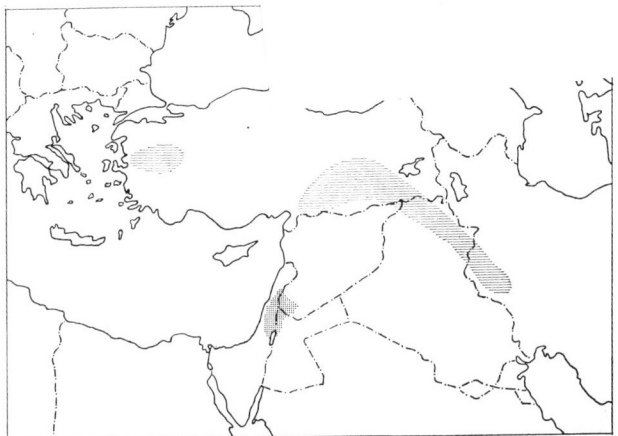

Fig. 3b. The distribution of wild barley. *After Harlan and Zohany.*

possibly consume in a year. Such activities, together with hunting and fishing, would explain how people like the Natufians, or the inhabitants of Tell Mureybat on the Euphrates in Syria, would have been able to settle in one spot without cultivation or domestication.

Wheat and barley were grown together at all early Neolithic sites. Both were fundamental to the new economy; their grains are highly nutritious and can easily be stored, the return is high and the labour

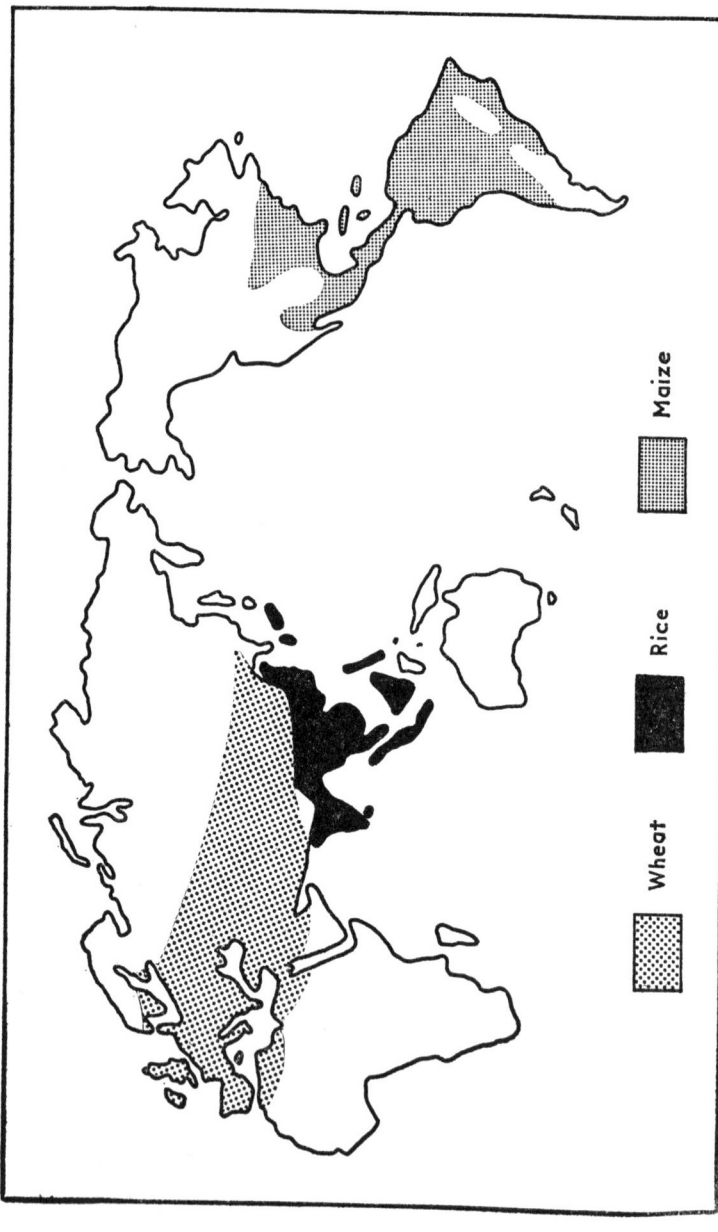

Fig. 4. The three great cereal areas of the world: the distribution of cultivated wheat, rice and maize in 1,500 A.D. *After Wissler.*

involved is seasonal, allowing leisure for other occupations. Deliberate selection of the best seed for sowing and accidental crossing of varieties produced grains very much larger than the seeds of wild grasses.

The three great cereal areas of the world are based on the cultivation of wheat, rice and maize, grains rich in energy-producing carbohydrates. The most ancient civilizations arose among the growers of wheat and barley in the Near and Middle East; later came the rice-growers of southern and eastern Asia and the maize-growers of Central America. For a long time the evolution of culture in these three areas was independent (Fig. 4). Thus the sweet potato, *Ipomoea batatas*, is the only American food-plant known to have passed into cultivation outside America in pre-Columbian times: maize, Irish potato (*Solanum tuberosum*), sunflower, tomato, French, lima and runner beans have attained their world-wide cultivation since then. Similarly, wheat, barley, rice and soya bean were unknown in America before that time.

The carbohydrate-yielding cereals are native to areas where protein-rich leguminous plants, or pulses, also grow wild. Oil-producing plants, such as flax, were also important, and various roots and fruit were cultivated in Neolithic times as well.

Cereals

WHEAT

The origin of the cultivated wheats has long been the subject of speculation and enquiry. Modern botanical and archaeological evidence suggests that the cultivation of both wheat and barley began in the Near East. The process of development from wild grasses to high-yielding modern wheats is imperfectly known, but it has involved gene mutations, hybridization and chromosome-doubling. This process, which has taken thousands of years, has been given direction through artificial selection by man as well as through natural selection under the diversity of climatic conditions to which the crop has been exposed during human migrations.

The cultivated species of wheat, *Triticum*, are classified in three groups: the diploid group with 2 sets of 7 chromosomes (consisting of einkorn alone); the tetraploid group with 4 sets of 7 chromosomes (including emmer and several others); and the hexaploid group with

6 sets of 7 chromosomes (comprising bread wheat, *T. aestivum*; club wheat, *T. compactum*; and spelt, *T. spelta*).

One of the basic wild wheats of the Near and Middle East is the diploid *Triticum boeoticum* (Fig. 5*a*). It gave rise to einkorn, *T. monococcum* (Fig. 5*b*), in which the ear did not shatter so readily and was therefore easier to harvest. Since brittle ears fall to the ground, the tougher ones are naturally harvested and when sown, they are selected automatically for this feature. Domestic species thus differ from wild prototypes without necessarily involving genetic mutations in the early stages of agriculture. The centre of selection for einkorn (Pl. II*a*) was probably south-eastern Anatolia. Einkorn was introduced to Europe by the first farmers, but it has now almost disappeared except in mountainous regions where no other wheat is hardy enough to yield a satisfactory crop. To account for finds at Jarmo and Ali Kosh, one must suppose that the wild prototype formerly grew further east than at present.

The tetraploid *T. dicoccoides* also grows wild in the Middle East, but has a more restricted distribution than *T. boeoticum*. Like the latter it is essentially a plant of the uplands, but it will not tolerate cold conditions or poor soil to the same extent. *T. dicoccoides* (Fig. 6*a*) gave rise to the cultivated tetraploid emmer, *T. dicoccon* (Fig. 6*b*). Emmer is far more valuable as a food crop than einkorn; it has been found at nearly all early Neolithic sites in the Middle East and in Egypt, as well as at the Swiss lake-side villages. In north-western Europe, emmer lingered on until well after the birth of Christ; indeed it was cultivated in Britain until the sixth century A.D.

Carbonized grains and clay impressions of spikelets of a form of emmer were recovered at Jarmo, Iraq, dating from the later half of the pre-pottery Neolithic period, about 6,000 B.C. (Pl. II). The wheat grains are nearer to the wild *T. dicoccoides* than to true cultivated emmer and evidently represent an early stage in the evolution of the crop. The Jarmo material shows considerable variation, whereas the cultivated emmer of other localities and later periods, having been subjected to longer selection, is comparatively uniform. During the 5th millennium, farmers began to cultivate the alluvial plains of Lower Iraq. Emmer apparently became well adapted to the irrigated land, while einkorn did not. The same situation occurred also in Egypt.

Primitive kinds of cultivated wheat, such as einkorn and emmer, which most nearly resemble the wild forms, are hairy and dark

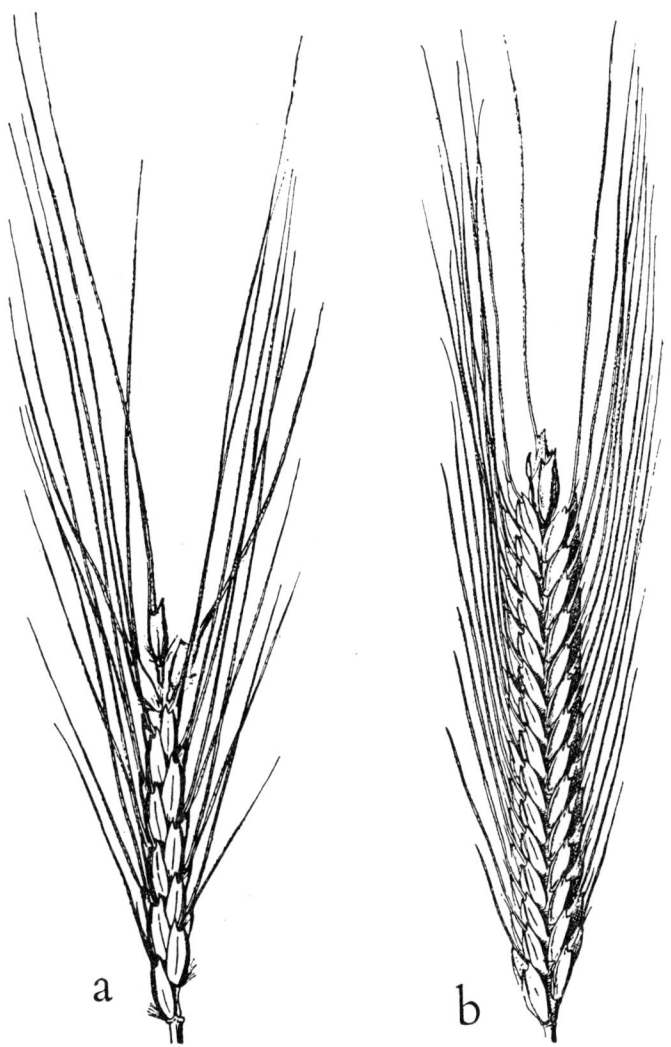

Fig. 5. (a) The diploid wheat *Triticum boeoticum*, wild ancestor of einkorn;
(b) *T. monococcum*, cultivated einkorn. Approx. nat. size. *After E. Schiemann.*

coloured; their seeds scatter and fall soon after they are ripe, since the
fragile axis of the spike breaks easily. These are called hulled wheats or
glume wheats, since the stiff, close-fitting glumes do not release the
kernels when threshed; this is an advantage to the plant in the wild

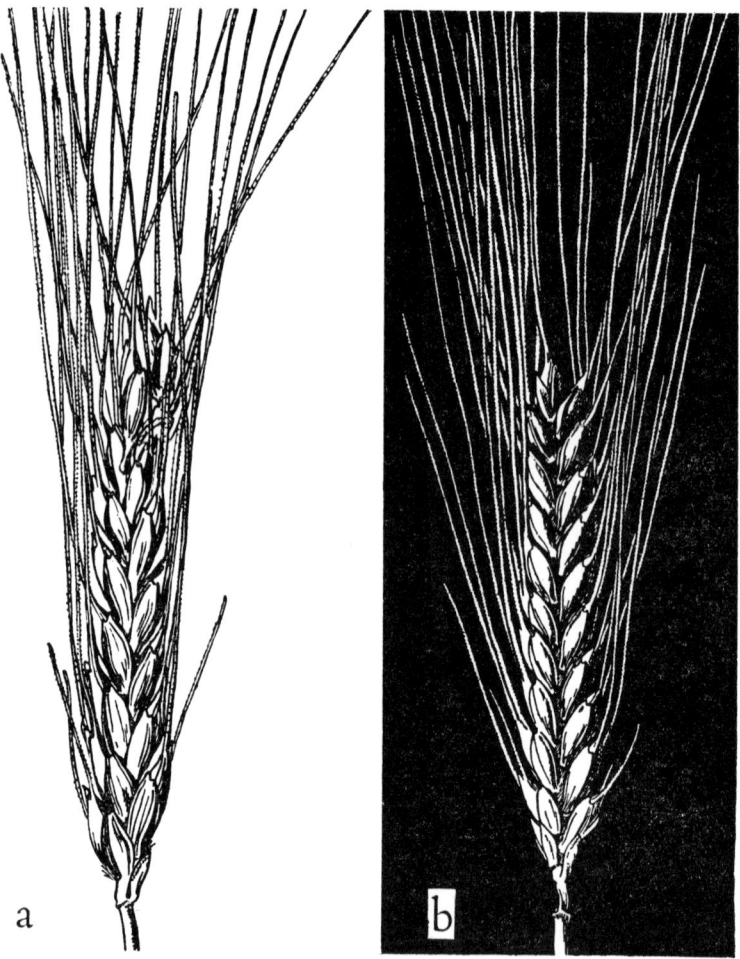

Fig. 6. (a) The tetraploid wheat *Triticum dicoccoides*, wild ancestor of emmer; (b) *T. dicoccon*, cultivated emmer. ⅔. *After E. Schiemann.*

state, but is obviously a disadvantage to the farmer. When the glumes remain associated with the grains, such as at Jarmo and other early Neolithic sites, positive identification of the species is comparatively easy. More highly cultivated forms have the grains loose within the spikelets at maturity and can be detached readily from the chaff; these are known as naked wheats.

In general, the hexaploid bread wheat, *T. aestivum*, did not become important before the Iron Age, though apparently it was grown at Knossos about 6,000 B.C. and soon after at Çatal Hüyük, together with emmer and einkorn. The variety of crops grown at this site around 6,000 B.C. is amazing: as well as the three varieties of wheat, the inhabitants grew naked barley, pea, vetch and bitter vetch; vegetable oil was obtained from crucifers, almonds, acorns and pistachio, while the great quantities of hackberry (*Celtis*) seeds suggest the production of hackberry wine.

No wild hexaploid wheat is known and the cultivated varieties are believed to have been derived from tetraploids (the emmer group) by hybridization with a diploid grass, *Aegilops*, and by chromosome doubling. The hexaploid group also includes spelt, *T. spelta*, which was perhaps first grown during the Bronze Age, and club wheat, *T. compactum*, found sporadically in Neolithic contexts but to a large extent only in the Swiss lake-side villages. Hexaploid wheats were grown in India soon after 3,000 B.C. and in China about a thousand years later.

BARLEY

Barley also grows wild almost ubiquitously in the Near and Middle East, under many different ecological conditions, and overlaps with the two varieties of wild wheat in the region of Syria. Possibly barley first came into cultivation accidentally as a weed in the wheat fields, and it is found at Neolithic sites in the same early levels as wheat. There are two main groups; two-row barley and six-row barley. The two-row barleys are represented by *Hordeum spontaneum* (Fig. 7a), growing wild in the Middle East, and *H. distichum*, known only in cultivation. The six-row form *H. agriocrithon* (Fig. 7b), first discovered in eastern Tibet, was later identified also in Israel. Formely believed to be wild, it is now considered to be a secondary derivative, resulting from occasional spontaneous hybridization between wild two-row and cultivated six-row forms. The two-row *H. spontaneum* is thus apparently the sole wild ancestor of all cultivated barleys. In cultivation six-row forms are represented by the dense-eared *H. hexastichum* and the loose-eared *H. tetrastichum*.

The earliest cultivated barley is known from Beidha, Çatal Hüyük and Jarmo; it is very like the wild *H. spontaneum*, differing from it only in the bigger grains and tougher axis (Pl. III). Six-row barley replaced the two-row form as a result of mutations after agriculture moved to the irrigated alluvial plains. In the grain storage pits of the Fayum, Egypt, dating from about 4,500 B.C., most of the barley was six-row; two-row barley was also reported, but its identification has been doubted. Six-row barley of the dense-eared type was commonly grown by the Danubian farmers and in late Neolithic Europe; carbonized grains preserved in mud at the Neolithic lake-side villages of Switzerland are mainly of this type. At the present day it is only cultivated in a few areas, *i.e.* in the Alps, central Sweden and the Faroes. The more evolved lax-eared form *H. tetrastichum*, now widely cultivated, was grown in Neolithic times in Britain and Denmark. As in the case of wheat, there are both hulled and naked kinds of barley; the crops grown during the Neolithic were nearly always hulled, for example at Jarmo, though naked barley was cultivated in parts of northern Europe in prehistoric times.

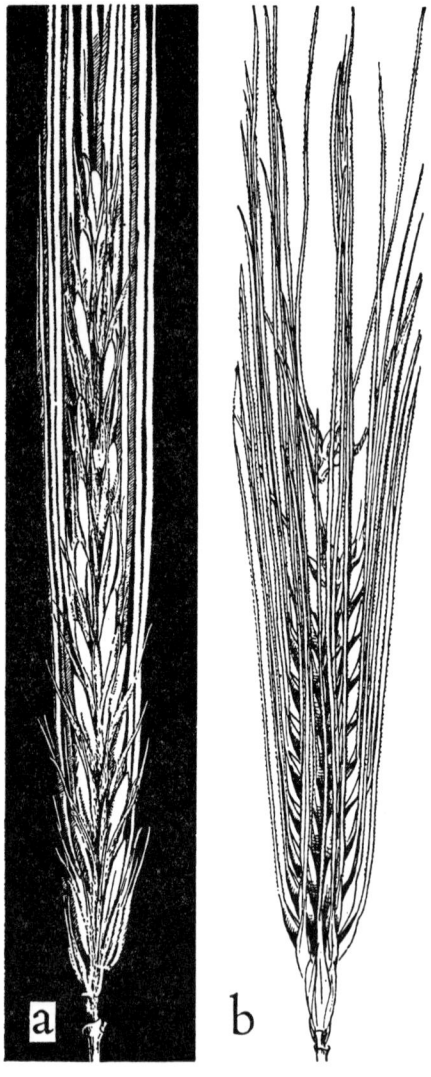

Fig. 7. (a) Wild two-row barley, *Hordeum spontaneum*; (b) Six-row barley, *H. agrio-crithon*. ⅔. *After E. Schiemann.*

PLANTING AND HARVESTING GRAIN

Grain was planted at first in small plots, thus

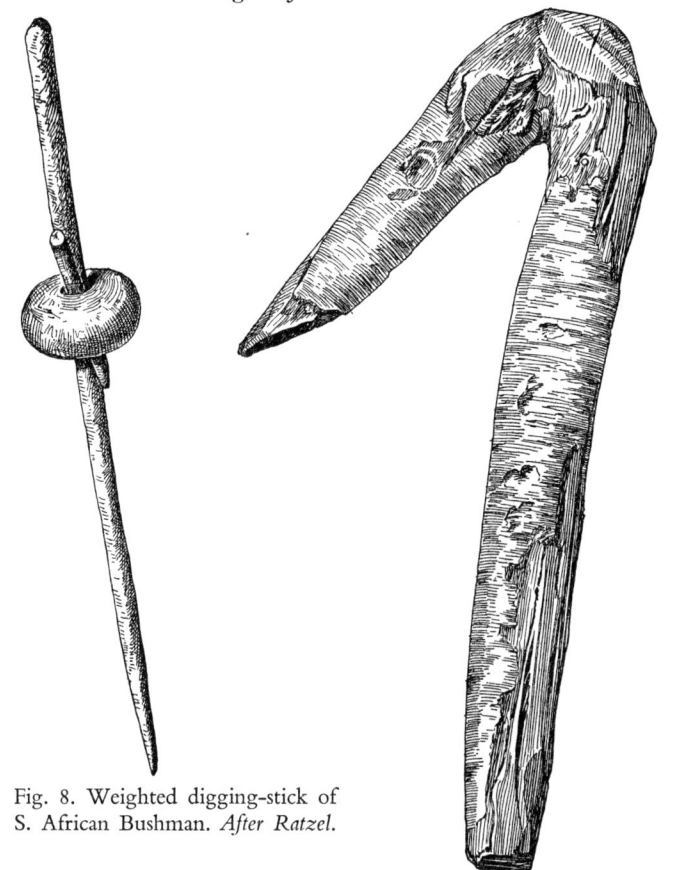

Fig. 8. Weighted digging-stick of
S. African Bushman. *After Ratzel.*

Fig. 9. Wooden hoe cut from forked branch. Kahun, Egypt, *c.* 2,000 B.C. ⅓.
By courtesy of Dept. of Egyptology, University College, London.

beginning as a garden rather than a field crop. In dry open country the
ground was broken up by means of a weighted digging-stick (Fig. 8),
or, when it was relatively soft, with a wooden hoe cut from a forked
branch (Fig. 9). Stone-bladed hoes were used in some areas, for
example at Hassuna in Iraq. The primitive wooden hoe persisted along-
side more elaborate types throughout the Middle and New Kingdoms
in Ancient Egypt and is still used by some hill tribes in central Africa
and India. Where grain was grown in forest clearings, as it was in
many parts of Europe, the Neolithic farmers may not have used

digging-sticks or hoes, but harrowed in the seed among the loose ashes of the burnt forest, as the Finnish peasants did until quite recently. Not until the plough was invented could heavy clay soils be cultivated. The earliest plough was no more than a hoe drawn through the ground, at first perhaps by a man with a rope, later by oxen. Ox-drawn ploughs were in use in parts of the Middle East by 3,000 B.C., but they did not appear in Europe until more than 1,500 years later.

On a private experimental plot at Kew, einkorn and emmer were grown from 1953 to 1955 by W. T. Stearn under 'Neolithic' conditions, using a digging stick and a light wooden hoe almost identical with the one shown in Fig. 9, which he made without the use of metal tools. With such primitive implements it was only possible to dig light soils, to a depth of 9 inches, and the eradication of deeply rooted weeds proved very difficult. This explains the stunted growth of the plants produced in this experiment, which are no doubt similar to those of Neolithic times.

The ancient Egyptian method of harvesting, as portrayed in tomb paintings (Fig. 10), shows that the head of corn was held in the hand and cut high on the stalk, using flint sickle blades hafted in wood or

Fig. 10. Ancient Egyptian method of harvesting. The head of corn was held in the hand and cut high on the stalk. Painting in Tomb of Mereruka, *c.* 2,300 B.C. *After Duell.*

bone (Fig. 11). This method is suitable for hulled wheat or barley, but with highly evolved naked forms it would have led to the grains being scattered on the ground.

MILLET

Two kinds of millet have been found at Neolithic sites in Europe: broomcorn millet, *Panicum miliaceum*, and Italian millet, *Setaria italica*, of which the former is the more common. Italian millet is related to the wild green millet, *Setaria viridis*, which occurs as a weed in southern Europe and North Africa. The origins of broomcorn millet are uncertain, but it is very similar to the Abyssinian wild *Panicum callosum*.

There is only one possible early find of broomcorn millet: in the aceramic levels of Argissa, in Greek Thessaly, where the carbonized grains resemble cultivated forms. Otherwise its earliest known appearance is about 3,000 B.C. at Jemdt Nasr in Iraq. It was the main crop during Neolithic times in the Far East, particularly China, therefore ranking in importance with corn as a basis of early civilization.

The millets grown extensively by primitive agriculturists in tropical Africa today belong to the genera *Elusine* (finger millet) and *Pennisetum* (pearl or bullrush millet). Probably both have an African origin.

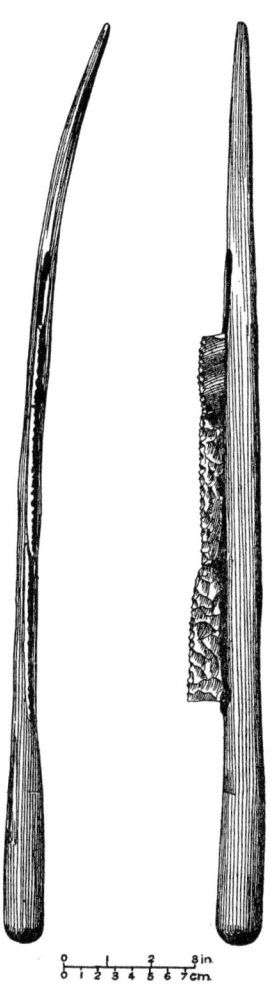

Fig. 11. Flint sickle-blades hafted in wooden handle, Neolithic, Fayum, Egypt. *After Caton-Thompson and Gardner.*

SORGHUM

The sorghums are cereals of ancient cultivation in tropical Africa south of the Sahara, particularly in regions of low rainfall. A few forms were introduced into India, via southern Arabia, and thence into the Mediterranean region in historic times.

OATS AND RYE

Wild oats were gathered at Beidha and Ali Kosh, but the large grains in aceramic levels at Achilleion, Greek Thessaly, were presumably cultivated. Otherwise there is very little evidence that either oats or rye were cultivated before the first millennium B.C., when rye was grown particularly in Germany, oats in Germany, Switzerland and Denmark. Both plants probably first appeared as weeds in wheat fields.

More than one species of wild oats may have given rise to the cultivated varieties. The most widely cultivated, *Avena sativa*, probably arose from the wild *A. fatua* of western Asia, North Africa and eastern Europe. Having a wider range of tolerance than wheat, it was probably carried northwards as a weed of the wheat fields and then selected for growing as an independent crop where conditions were unfavourable for wheat. Cultivated varieties of rye probably arose in the same way from weed-rye of Asia Minor, which in turn was derived from the wild *Secale ancestrale*. Weed plants, while not in the first place grown deliberately as crops, are subject to the same processes of selection for adaptability to cultivated conditions as the crop plants with which they are associated.

RICE

The growing of rice (Fig. 4), the staple diet of tropical countries, involves more continuous labour than grain cultivation. It evolved from the wild *Oryza sativa* native to the East Indies. Probably rice was cultivated in India earlier than in China, where it appeared during the late Neolithic, about 2,000 B.C. Millet was the main crop grown during this period in China, but imprints of rice husks were identified in pottery from the Neolithic settlement of Yang Shao Tsun.

MAIZE

Fossil maize pollen was found at a depth of 200 feet in borings beneath Mexico City dating from the Last Interglacial period, at least 80,000 years ago, and these pollen grains are scarcely distinguishable from those of modern maize. But no living wild plant can be identified with certainty as the original ancestor of cultivated maize, *Zea mays*, the cereal on which the pre-Columbian civilizations of Peru and central America were based (Fig. 4). The explanation probably is that wild plants would not have been able to survive the effects of certain characters of cultivated maize conveyed to them by wind pollination. Cultivated maize is unique among the cereal grasses in that the terminal male 'tassel' is widely separated from the lateral female 'ears'; the kernels are enclosed in leaf sheaths and there is no mechanism for the dispersal of seeds, with the result that cultivated maize cannot reproduce itself without man's intervention. In breeding experiments in the U.S.A., types of a primitive nature, with a terminal inflorescence bearing both male and female flowers and very small cobs, were obtained by crossing podcorn and popcorn which had isolated primitive features. The resultant dwarf forms, which can compete with other vegetation, must approximate very closely to the early cultivated forms of maize.

The oldest known remains of maize come from Coxcatlán Cave in the state of Puebla, Mexico, dated by radiocarbon to about 5,000 B.C. The tiny cobs are uniform in size, suggesting that they are either from wild maize or maize in the earliest stages of domestication. Cobs from Bat Cave, New Mexico, dating from about 3,600 B.C., are still very small.

It seems that maize may not have been the earliest plant to be cultivated in the New World; gourds, lima beans and squashes were probably grown in Mexico before 5,000 B.C.

BREAD AND BEER

Grain crops have many uses. In Neolithic times, cereal grains were probably first parched—'popped'—in ovens, then ground and made into gruel. Clay ovens, baked into the floor, occur in pre-pottery levels at Jarmo (Pl. XVII). Large querns for grinding are common at most Neolithic sites in the Middle East, particularly at Jericho. Unleavened biscuits are likely to have been made in Neolithic times, but the earliest evidence of leavened bread is from the beginning of the Bronze Age; carbonized pieces of 'bread' were found at the later Swiss lakeside villages.

When gruel stands for any length of time it is liable to ferment and this undoubtedly led to brewing as well as baking. Beer can be made from most cereals and is likely to be as old as agriculture itself.

Evidence from the Fayum, where conditions of preservation are excellent, show that elaborate measures were taken to store the precious grain. It was kept in large silage pits lined with basketry, and would have ensured a plentiful supply of food and drink until the next harvest.

Leguminous Plants

Beans, peas and lentils are fairly common at early Neolithic sites, though generally it is impossible to say if they were wild or cultivated. It seems probable that they would have been widely grown owing to the large size of their seed, or pulses, their ease of storage, and their high protein content. Many of the smaller leguminous plants growing as weeds may have passed into cultivation. The small-seeded broad bean of Neolithic Europe, *Vicia faba* var. *minor*, known as the 'Celtic bean', may be descended from *Vicia pliniana* of North Africa, whence it reached Spain. The 'Celtic bean' also spread through Europe from the south-east with the Danubian culture, and still survives in eastern Europe and Spain.

While beans thrived in the colder parts of Europe, peas could only be cultivated under warmer conditions. The field pea, *Pisum sativum arvense*, is probably descended from the wild purple pea, *P. elatus*, distributed from the Mediterranean to India. It was grown at Çatal Hüyük at least by 6,500 B.C.; at Jarmo in Iraq; and at Merimde in Egypt (about 4,500 B.C.).

Lentils, *Lens esculenta*, are derived from the black lentil *L. nigricans* of the Mediterranean and countries east of the Himalayas. Larger seeds show that they were cultivated in Turkey and Egypt in Neolithic times and at Khafaje in Iraq about 3,000 B.C. They were introduced into Europe by Danubian farmers.

Oil-producing Plants

Oil-producing plants were grown to supplement animal fats for food and also for lighting purposes. The chief oil plants are olives, sesame, the castor oil plant, rape and flax. Flax, *Linum usitatissimum* (Fig. 12), is descended from *L. bienne*, which grows wild in the Kurdish foothills; it was particularly important not only as a source of oil from its seeds (linseed), but also for the sake of its fibres for weaving. Cloth impressions dating from the pre-pottery period have survived on balls of

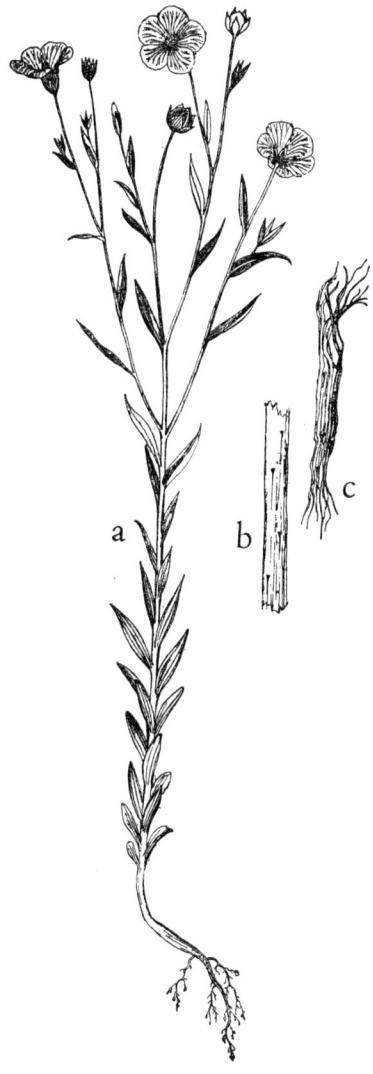

Fig. 12. (a) Flax, *Linum usitatissimum*, ⅓. (b) part
of stem stripped of leaves (note leaf-bases)
slightly enlarged; (c) the same, retted. *a. After
Sowerby; b–c, after R. L. Davis.*

clay at Jarmo, and pieces of linen have been preserved at the Fayum
(*c.* 4,500 B.C.). A different species of flax was grown in the Alpine
region during the third millennium B.C. Its seeds were small, like those
of plants grown in the foothills of the Middle East (linseeds from the
alluvial plains were much larger).

Fruit

Carbonized apples were found at Çatal Hüyük (6,500 B.C.) and other
orchard fruits were grown in the Middle East during the fourth millennium. Remains of dates and olives have been found at a number of
Neolithic sites and the vine grape was grown at this time in both Syria
and Egypt. Probably grape cultivation began in the mountainous
region of north Mesopotamia, Syria and Palestine, where vines grow
wild. It reached Italy during the first millennium B.C.

Carbonized apples, some cut in half for drying, were found at Neolithic Swiss villages. They are larger than the wild crab, implying that
they were cultivated, and traces of anthocyanin indicate that they were
a red variety. There are many species of wild crab apples, but the
ancestor of the cultivated types is *Malus pumila* of south-western Asia.

3
Domestication of Animals

Sheep and goats were first domesticated in the homeland of their wild ancestors, the Middle East. When wheat and barley were first cultivated in this area, it may be that animals gradually became attached to man for protection and for the food he was able to offer them. There is no certain evidence as to whether stock-keeping or plant cultivation came first: very likely they arose at more or less the same time in different areas. In some cases hunters may have taken to herding stock, in others the reaping of wild cereals probably led to their cultivation. Dogs may have been the first animals to be domesticated, by Mesolithic hunters; at present, however, the earliest known date for any domesticated animal is 8,900 B.C. for sheep. Both sheep and goats were kept by proto-Neolithic peoples. Cattle and pigs were reared slightly later; probably they became associated with man through raiding his crops. It is clear from such sites as Jarmo that mixed farming began very early; stubble left after reaping would have provided good grazing for animals which would, in turn, benefit the crops by their manure.

Animals were first valued for their meat and hides; then, as they became more docile, they would have been milked and finally they were used as pack animals. By killing off the wildest rams and bulls and preserving the more amenable, selective breeding would have begun. Man encourages various characters arising through mutations which, in the wild state, would be unfavourable and which would die out as the result of natural selection. Examples are docile behaviour, conspicuously coloured coats, and long hair.

Many experiments must have been made in trying to tame various kinds of animals which were to prove unsuitable for domestication. The Egyptians tried to tame antelopes, gazelles, monkeys and hyaenas without much success.

The ass *Equus asinus* was domesticated in Egypt from the Nubian wild ass. It was the earliest pack animal, and its relative, the onager *E. hemionus hemippus*, was harnessed to wheeled vehicles in Mesopotamia about 3,000 B.C. The horse, the descendant of the now extinct tarpan, was domesticated probably in north-western Asia, and spread across the western world in the Bronze Age, during the first half of the second millennium B.C.

The only domesticated animals important in Neolithic times, however, were the four food animals which still provide man's staple diet— sheep, goats, pigs and cattle—and also the dog, as companion and hunter's aid.

Dogs

A date of 8,400 B.C. for domesticated dogs at Idaho, U.S.A., needs confirmation. Apart from this, it seems that dogs were first tamed from wolves by Mesolithic peoples in Northern Europe from about 7,500 B.C. Most authorities now agree that the so-called 'dog' from Natufian sites in the Middle East was the Asiatic wolf, *Canis lupus arabs*, which is smaller than the European wolf. The relatively wide muzzle of these animals was thought to show the effects of domestication, but there is certainly much variation in this feature among wolves. In the aceramic levels at Jericho, which follow immediately after the Natufian levels, there is considerable size variation in the canid remains. Crowded and displaced teeth in domesticated animals are generally due to the diet, but at Jericho it is possible that such animals were tamed wolves rather than fully domesticated dogs. At Jarmo, clay figurines from aceramic levels portray a small dog with curled-up tail, a characteristic of pariahs; here there can be no possible confusion with wolves.

Apparently domesticated dogs (though again there is a possibility that they were small wolves) have been identified at the Mesolithic site of Star Carr in Yorkshire, dated by radiocarbon to 7,538±350 B.C. This date has a rather large margin of possible error, but there is little doubt that dogs were kept by the Maglemosians of Denmark about 6,500 B.C.

It seems likely that dogs were domesticated independently in Europe and Western Asia from European and Arabian wolves. Others, including the pariah dogs of India and the Australian dingo, were apparently derived from the Indian wolf.

The scavenging habits of wolves must have led them into hunters' camps. They may have been encouraged to do so as useful disposers of rubbish and puppies may have been kept as pets. Once tamed, dogs

would have helped hunters to track wounded game and later on, in
Neolithic times, they would have assisted in driving and cornering
herds of goats and sheep. Skeletons from Neolithic settlements in
Britain and Switzerland show that some of the dogs stood about 18
inches at the shoulder (Pl. IV).

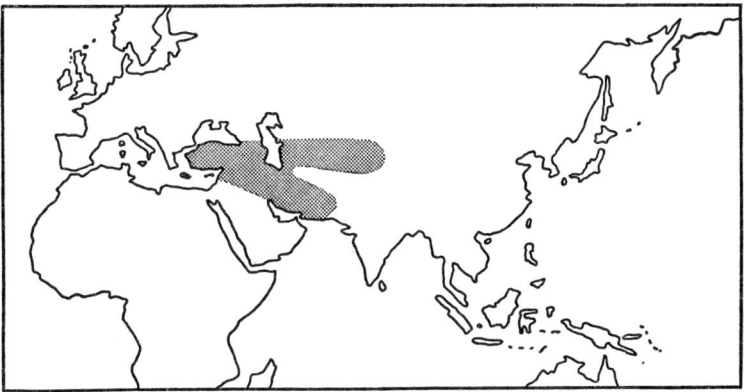

Fig. 13. Distribution of wild goat, *Capra*.

Goats

It is not at all easy to separate sheep from goats when their frag-
mentary remains are found with archaeological material. One way of
doing it is by their metacarpals—but needless to say, these small bones
are not always found. Teeth, which are the remains most commonly
found, are not diagnostic. Luckily, however, horn-cores are. The bony
core is about two-thirds of the length of the horn sheath, which generally perishes in a short time. In primitive forms of goat, the horns of
both sexes were originally scimitar-like, but in more advanced
domesticated types they generally rise in a wide, open spiral above the
head. In the case of sheep, the horns of rams are nearly always in a spiral
while those of ewes are either short points or may be absent altogether.

Horn-cores are not always found in archaeological deposits either,
and other means have to be found to distinguish wild from domesticated
animals. One method which often proves helpful concerns the proportion of bones of adult and immature specimens. A high percentage
of remains of young animals suggests that they had been killed at a

certain season, probably when food was in short supply in winter or
early spring.

The earliest evidence of domesticated goats comes from aceramic
levels at Jericho, Jarmo (Pl. VI*a*) and Ali Kosh. At Ali Kosh, most of the
remains of goats from the earliest phase (before 6,000 B.C.) were of
males less than three years old. Domesticated goats were derived from
the bezoar, *Capra hircus aegagrus*, which still lives wild in the mountains
of south-western Asia (Pl. V; Fig. 13). The bezoar has scimitar-like
horns, curved in a vertical plane. The horns of the early Neolithic
domesticated goats are similar, but they are flatter in cross-section and
sometimes show an incipient twist (*Fig.* 14*a*, *b*). By the time of the
pottery levels they show an appreciable twist, which became still
more pronounced during the Bronze Age (Fig. 14*c*). One of the best
known early representations of a goat is the so-called 'ram caught in
a thicket' from Ur, about 2,500 B.C.

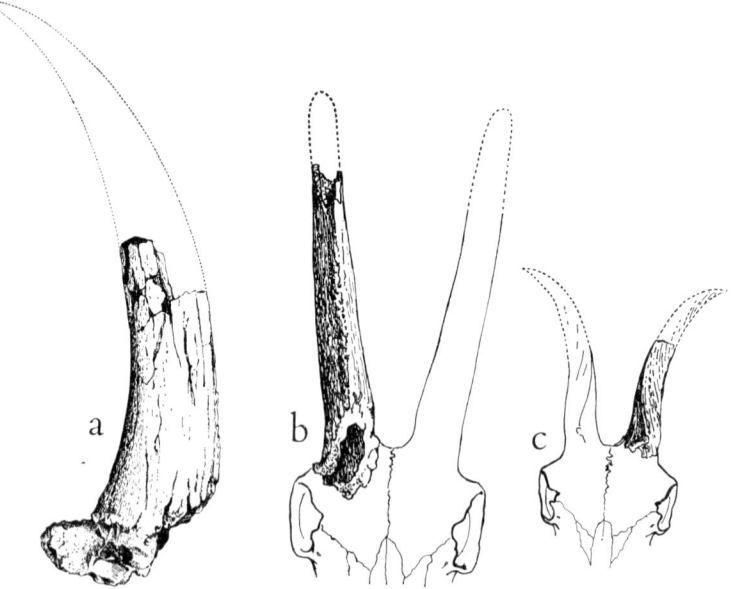

Fig. 14. (a) Restored horn-core of semi-domesticated goat, pre-pottery Neolithic, Jericho; (b) the same, front view; (c) restored horn-cores of domesticated
goat, showing smaller size and marked twist, Bronze Age, Jericho. 1/6. *Based on
Zeuner.*

Sheep

Earliest of all domesticated animals, as we have seen, are sheep at Zawi Chemi Shanidar in northern Iraq, about 8,900 B.C. The reason for believing them to be domesticated lies in the high proportion of young animals. The average for kills of wild animals one year or less is not more than 25 per cent and this is the proportion throughout the long sequence of Palaeolithic deposits in Shanidar cave. Yet at the time of the proto-Neolithic village of Zawi Chemi Shanidar, the percentage of yearlings rose to 60 per cent. In contrast to Zawi Chemi Shanidar, during the earliest phase at Ali Kosh sheep were less important than goats, but in later levels sheep became more numerous. At Nea Nikomedeia in Greece, 47 per cent of the goat and sheep bones were those of immature animals. This site, dated to 5,600 B.C. by radiocarbon, provides the earliest evidence for domesticated sheep, goats, pigs and cattle in Europe. Remains of woollen cloth found in carbonized form at Çatal Hüyük shows that domesticated sheep were kept there slightly earlier.

Domesticated sheep are believed to have been derived mainly from the mouflon, of which there are three forms living wild in Europe and Asia. The true mouflon comprises the European *Ovis musimon* and the western Asiatic *O. orientalis* (Pl. V). The former probably once lived wild on the continent of Europe, but now only a few survive in Corsica and Sardinia; *O. orientalis* still lives in Cyprus and Turkey. The third form of mouflon, *O. vignei*, is often known as the urial (Fig. 15) and is

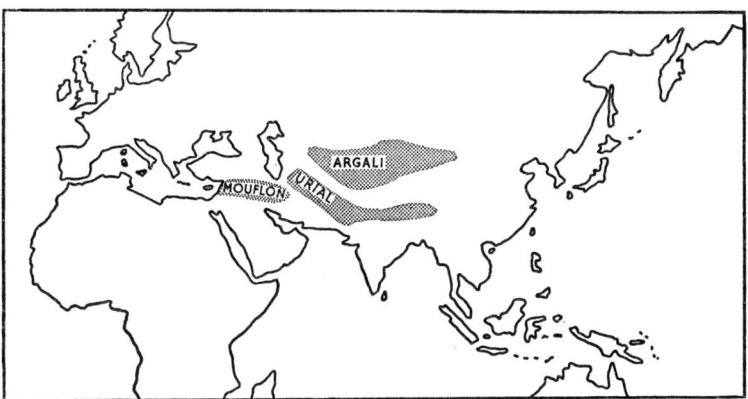

Fig. 15. Distribution of wild sheep, *Ovis*.

generally larger and paler in colour than the others. The argali of central
Asia, O. *ammon*, probably made little contribution to domesticated
forms of sheep except locally in the mountains of central Asia.

An interesting question is whether living 'wild' sheep do, in fact,
represent the original prototype, or whether they have interbred with
domesticated sheep and become feral. Bones that can be certainly
identified as those of sheep have rarely, if ever, been found at Palaeolithic sites and apparently these animals were not hunted. Yet soon after
9,000 B.C. they are well represented. One suggestion is that sheep are
the result of human selection on a common 'goat-sheep' stock.

Some domesticated sheep of western Europe, such as the Soay sheep
of the Outer Hebrides, seem to be direct descendants of the true
mouflon and are probably very similar to the earliest domesticated
sheep. A breed derived from the urial was introduced into Europe from
Asia in Neolithic times and is known as the Turbary sheep. Its goat-like
horns have been recognized at the Swiss lake-side villages of around
2,500 B.C. and similar sheep have been identified at early Neolithic
sites in Britain, for instance Windmill Hill (*c.* 3,000 B.C.). Survivors of
this strain are believed to be the Drente breed of the Netherlands and
both Merino and Norfolk Black Face sheep may have urial ancestry.

Selective breeding must have produced a woolly fleece to replace
the coarse hair of the wild ancestor in quite early times, for artists in
Mesopotamia from the fourth millennium B.C. onwards clearly depict
this characteristic.

Pigs

The domesticated pig is descended from the common wild boar,
Sus scrofa scrofa (Pl. VII) of Europe, Asia and North Africa (Fig. 16).
Among the oldest known remains of domesticated pigs are those from
pottery levels of early Neolithic sites such as Jarmo—neither pigs nor
domesticated cattle have yet been found in aceramic levels. Earliest
known are the domesticated pigs from Cayönü in S.W. Anatolia;
there are also many remains from sites in the Crimea. One sign of
domestication in pigs is a reduction of the tooth row, particularly
in the length of the third molar. Reduced third molars first appear
in the pigs of pottery levels at Jarmo and Jericho. The evidence
for domesticated pigs at Nea Nikomedeia is particularly strong, since
not only are the third molars rather smaller than the average for wild

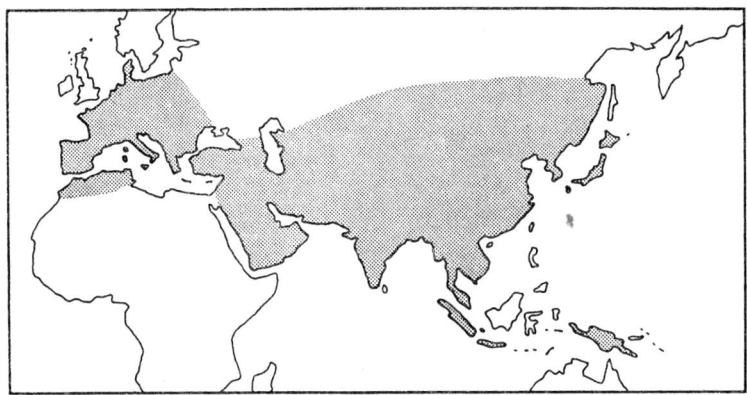

Fig. 16. Distribution of wild pig, *Sus scrofa.*

boars, but also no less than 90 per cent of the pig bones were those of yearlings.

At Çatal Hüyük, pigs seem to have been associated with death, presumably because of their scavenging habits. In some of the shrines, described on p. 61, human breasts were modelled in plaster round the lower jaw of a wild boar. No pig bones were found among the food debris and it is possible that the numerous taboos against eating pork, which still exist among certain peoples today, originated in Neolithic times.

The short snouts and rounded bodies of modern domestic pigs are due to selection of mutations. Modern breeds are derived mainly from *S. scrofa vittatus*, indigenous to south-eastern Asia. Pigs of this sub-species were kept by Chinese farmers in Neolithic times; they were, in fact, the only animals domesticated by them. In Europe, the Chinese breed seems to have largely replaced the form derived from *S. scrofa scrofa* during the eighteenth century A.D. An interesting piece of evidence supporting the Asiatic origin of modern domestic pigs is that lice found on European and American swine are the same as those on *S. scrofa vittatus*; but lice on the wild *S. scrofa scrofa* are of a different species. *S. scrofa vittatus* is more suited to being kept confined in styes; *S. scrofa scrofa* thrives better grubbing in woodlands.

Cattle

Domestic cattle are descended from the wild aurochs or urus, *Bos primigenius*, whose bones are common in deposits of Pleistocene age in

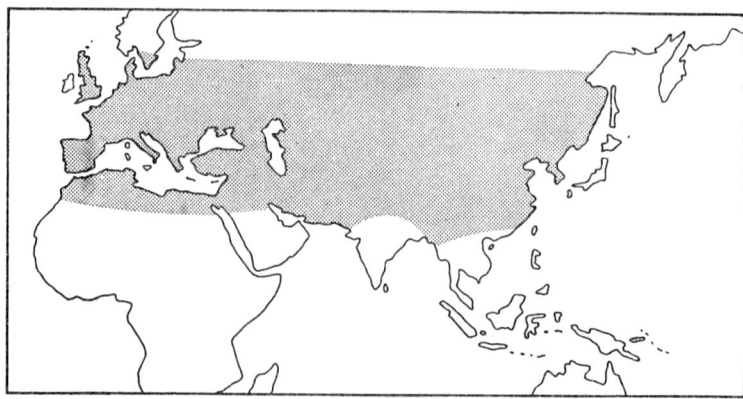

Fig. 17. Distribution of wild aurochs, *Bos primigenius*, during Pleistocene period.

Europe, Asia and North Africa (Fig. 17). The bulls were very large, standing up to 6 feet high at the shoulder, and had very long horns. The aurochs, which lived mostly in wooded country, was probably domesticated in Greece and Crete by about 6,000 B.C., and perhaps about the same time in Anatolia, if some of the abundant bones of cattle from Çatal Hüyük prove to belong to domesticated animals, as seems probable. At Nea Nikomedeia, about 6,000 B.C., 50 per cent of the bones of cattle were of immature animals, suggesting domestication. The earliest evidence from Asia apart from Anatolia comes from Tepe Sabz, Deh Luran, in Iranian Khuzistan, about 5,500 B.C. Remains of cattle from the Halafian site of Banahilk (5,000 B.C.) are much smaller than those of the wild aurochs and they were presumably domesticated. Owing to lack of attention and a restricted food supply, domesticated cattle gradually became smaller; but as they were originally subject to inter-breeding with the wild *Bos primigenius*, some of the Neolithic domesticated forms are barely distinguishable from their Pleistocene ancestors. On the other hand, there were apparently in Pleistocene times some wild forms reminiscent of modern cattle. An engraving of late Palaeolithic (Magdalenian) age from Teyjat in the Dordogne of a bull following a cow shows this clearly (Fig.18).

Domestic cattle of aurochs origin were introduced into western Europe by Neolithic farmers, spreading from the Danube basin. Although domestic cattle from British Neolithic sites had smaller bodies than the wild *B. primigenius*, their horns were often nearly as long as those of the aurochs of early post-Glacial times, but the immensely long horns of the Pleistocene *B. primigenius* did not persist after the end of the last glaciation. The bulls depicted in Minoan art were feral cattle (domesticated stock allowed to roam and which had reverted to a form resembling the ancestral aurochs).

Fig. 18. Upper Palaeolithic engraving, Teyjat, Dordogne. $\frac{1}{12}$. These examples of *Bos primigenius* in Pleistocene times appear to foreshadow modern cattle. *After Breuil.*

Short-horned cattle, the so-called *B. longifrons* or *brachyceros*, were domesticated in Europe by 3,000 B.C. but did not appear in Britain until late Bronze Age times (Fig. 19b). They were very much smaller than the Neolithic domesticated cattle; initially in fact it was almost a dwarf breed, although probably a descendant of *Bos primigenius*. *Bos longifrons* was almost certainly the result of a near-starvation diet and selection for small size and docility. The horn-cores are usually less than 3 inches in length, indicating that the horns themselves were under 6 inches long; hornless specimens have also been found.

Until very recently it was thought that the wild aurochs died out in Britain during Neolithic times, but its bones have now been found in the Cambridge area in peat attributed to the Early Bronze Age on the basis of pollen analysis. The aurochs survived far longer in some parts of Europe. The last known specimen was killed in Poland in 1627 (Pl. VIIIa). Recently 'bred-back' forms, believed to resemble the wild aurochs very closely, were reared by the brothers Heck, in the Berlin and Münich Zoos (Pl. VIIIb).

The white park cattle of Chillingham and formerly of Chartley, and the Duke of Hamilton's herd at Cadzow in Lanarkshire, are supposed to have been kept relatively pure since Roman times, when they were introduced from Italy to Britain (Pl. VI, *below*).

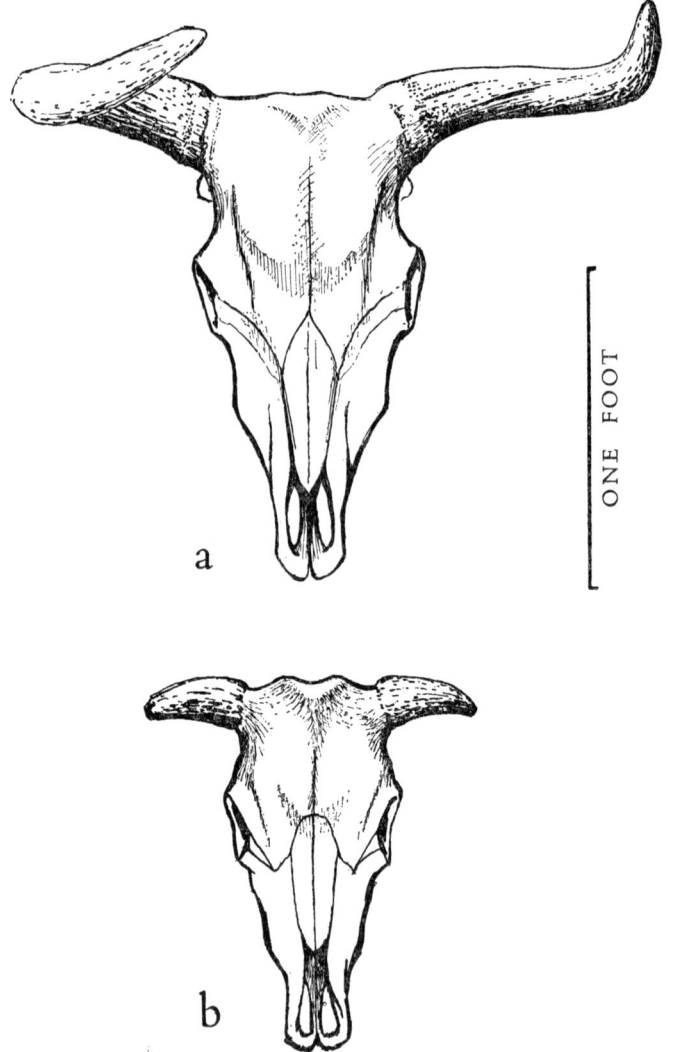

ONE FOOT

a

b

Fig. 19. (a) Horn-cores of presumably domesticated form of *Bos primigenius* (skull restored; one horn is abnormal in this individual); Neolithic, Maiden Castle, Dorset. (b) Horn-cores of domestic *B. longifrons* (skull restored); Early Iron Age, Chesterford, Essex. This breed of short-horned cattle did not appear in Britain until Late Bronze Age times.

It is possible that cattle were domesticated independently in several areas, for instance in Egypt and in India. Longhorn cattle were kept in Egypt at least from the fifth millennium B.C. and may have been domesticated from the local aurochs. The Pleistocene *Bos namadicus* of India may have given rise to humped zebu cattle, *B. taurus indicus*; both aurochs-like cattle and zebu are depicted on seals from Bronze Age sites such as Mohenjodaro. The lateral-horned zebu was introduced to Africa perhaps as early as 3,000 B.C. and much later, perhaps by 600 B.C., the short-horned zebu was brought to Africa and spread particularly after the expansion of the Arabs after the eighth century A.D.

Dairy farming may have been a relatively late development, but pictorial records show that it was practised in Mesopotamia at least as early as 3,000 B.C. There is no evidence of dairy farming before 1,000 B.C. in Europe. Cheese-making bowls have been found, dating from the later Bronze Age, with one large hole in the base and many small holes in the sides.

It is possible that religious motives played a part in the domestication of cattle. It is well known that bull sacrifice was important in the fertility cults of nearly all ancient civilizations and recent discoveries at Çatal Hüyük leave no doubt that such beliefs originated in Neolithic times, if not before. In many of the shrines, plaster 'goddesses' are associated with the horns of wild aurochs and in several instances the goddess is shown in the attitude of giving birth above a bull's head. There are also brick pillars incorporating auroch's horn-cores and huge bulls painted on the walls (see p. 51).

4
Axe-Trade and Forest Clearance

After the end of glacial times in Europe, about 8,000 B.C., dense forests began to spread over land which had formerly been tundra and steppe. From about 3,000 B.C. onwards, Neolithic farmers started to tackle the forests by burning and clearing with stone axes.

Axe-heads had already been pecked into shape and partly ground during the Mesolithic stage in northern Europe, but a technique characteristic of the Neolithic was fine polishing all over the implement. After the axe-head had been shaped by flaking, the surface was ground down by rubbing on a wetted stone slab; for example 'sarsen-stone' was used in southern England, with sand as an abrasive (Fig. 20a).

Flint Mining

Neolithic men apparently took great trouble to obtain the most suitable material for their axe-heads and it was traded over considerable distances. Good quality flint was particularly valued as it is hard yet comparatively easy to flake and grind. This material wherever it was accessible had, of course, been used for tools since the beginning of the Stone Age, but the large demand for axe-heads for forest clearance led to the exploitation of underground seams of flint and gave a new impetus to an age-old craft, which now became part of a well-organized industry.

Under Neolithic economy, food supplies were adequate to support specialized craftsmen. Thus flint miners supplied raw material to the axe-makers, who in turn passed their products on to traders.

Flint mining was carried out in England, France, Denmark, Sweden, Belgium, Poland, Portugal, Sicily and Egypt. The reddish yellow flint from Grand Pressigny in France was especially valued and was perhaps the most widely traded but was used mainly for making knives and sickles. Flat polished flint axe-heads showing an exceptionally high standard of workmanship are associated with early Neolithic burials in Scandinavia.

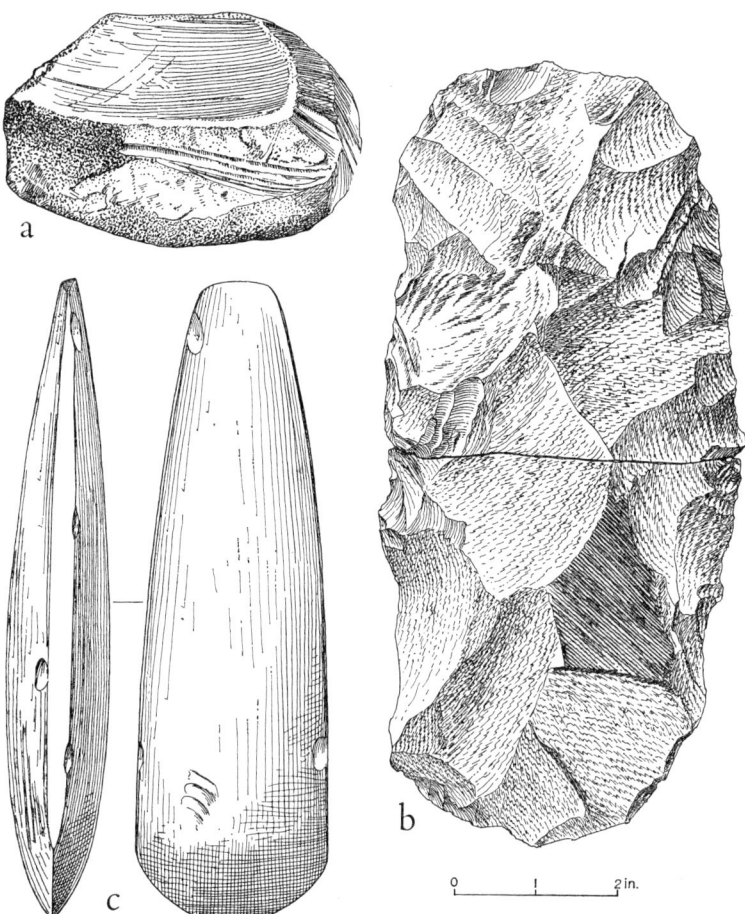

Fig. 20. (a) Sarsen stone used for polishing axe-heads. Farnham, Surrey. (b) Lava axe-head broken while being chipped into shape before polishing. Graig-Llwyd axe-factory, N. Wales. (c) Polished axe-head of greenish-grey volcanic tuff, probably from Langdale factory; Kelso, Scotland. *After K. P. Oakley.*

In England, the most important flint-mining areas were in the chalk country of Sussex and Norfolk. At Grime's Graves in Norfolk at least 34 acres were mined. The best flint layers were reached by sinking vertical shafts through the chalk and tunnelling horizontal galleries from them. Red deer antlers, with all tines except the 'brow' removed,

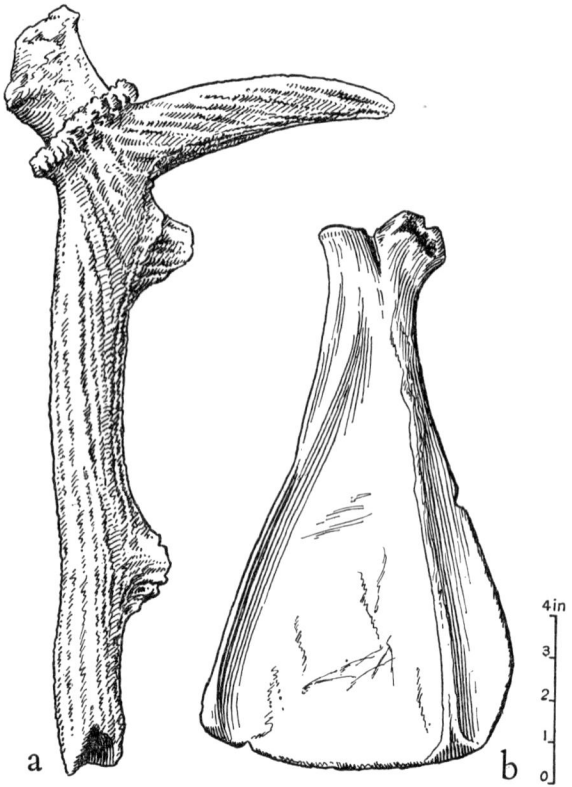

Fig. 21. (a) Antler pick used in flint mining, Grime's Graves, Norfolk. The point was probably hammered into natural joints to lever out blocks of chalk or flint. (b) Shoulder-blade of ox, used as shovel. Flint mine on Church Hill, Findon, Sussex. *By courtesy of the Worthing Museum.*

have been found in great quantities in the galleries (Fig. 21*a*). Evidently they were picks, and probably the points were hammered into natural joints and the intervening blocks levered out. Shovels made from shoulder-blades of cattle were also common (Fig. 21*b*).

Carbon-14 dates from Grime's Graves lie between 2,400 and 1,600 B.C. and others from flint mines in Sussex are even earlier, going back to about 3,000 B.C.

An experimental earthwork was built by the British Association in

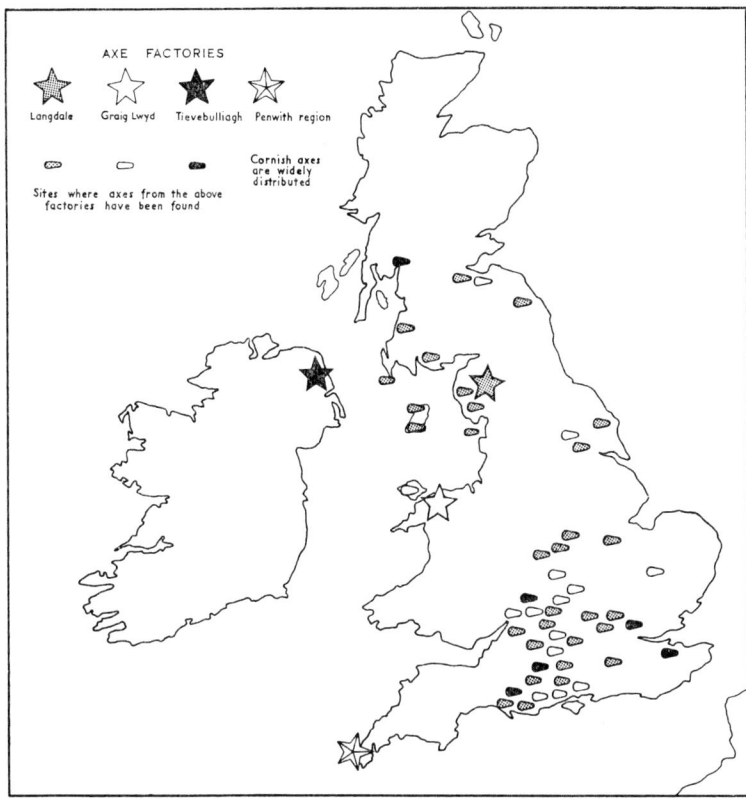

Fig. 22. Some of the main Neolithic stone axe-factories in Britain and the distribution of their products.

1960 at Overton Down, Wiltshire, with the object of studying the effects of time on buried materials. Part of the work was done by using only antler picks and shoulder-blade shovels, as in Neolithic times. The picks proved to be remarkably resilient and could be used either with a swinging blow, or by battering the tine into the chalk with a wooden mallet or large stone. None of the picks broke, although some of the points became splintered and all became shorter with use. The shoulder-blade shovels, on the other hand, were found to be inefficient and were best used to scrape the broken chalk into flat baskets for carrying from the ditch to the bank.

Axe-Factories in Britain

The geological structure of Britain determined the distribution of stone axe-factories. In south-east England, flint was obtainable by mining the chalk; but in the west and north, igneous rocks were used as material for polished axe-heads. On account of their greater toughness, 'green-stone' axes were evidently preferred to those of flint, for these were extensively traded into the flint country. Microscopical examination of thin sections cut from axe-heads found at innumerable localities all over the country has enabled geologists to trace their provenance and this has given much information about early trade routes (Fig. 22).

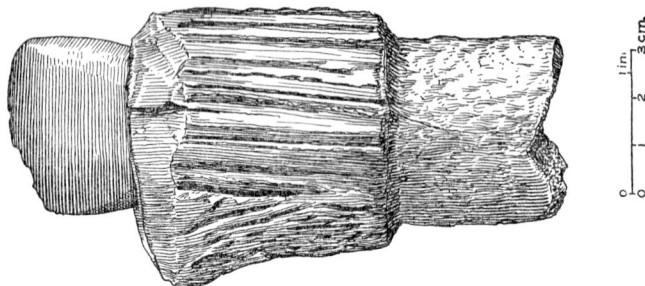

Fig. 23. Polished stone axe-head in antler sleeve, Neolithic lake-side village, Switzerland.

Axe-factories were situated near the coast, on either side of the Irish Sea. Among the most important centres of distribution were Great Langdale in Westmorland, Graig Lwyd in Caernarvon, Tievebulliagh Hill in County Antrim, and Penwith in Cornwall.

Axe-heads from the Great Langdale factory were traded along the coast and down rivers from Hampshire to the Firth of Forth (Fig. 20c). The material used was greenish volcanic tuff.

Fig. 24. Pollen diagram showing the effects of clearing forest for agriculture in Denmark *c.* 2,300 B.C., based on samples of pollen taken by boring in bogs. The width of the stippled areas represents the percentage of pollen of each species. As Neolithic farmers cleared the primeval forest with their polished stone axes, the pollen of big trees declined and was replaced by that of herbaceous plants (Stage 1). The great increase of birch pollen during Stage 2 suggests that clearings were burned. At the same time, cereals and weeds appeared. Finally (Stage 3) the big trees grew up again as the farmers moved on to new areas. *After Iversen.*

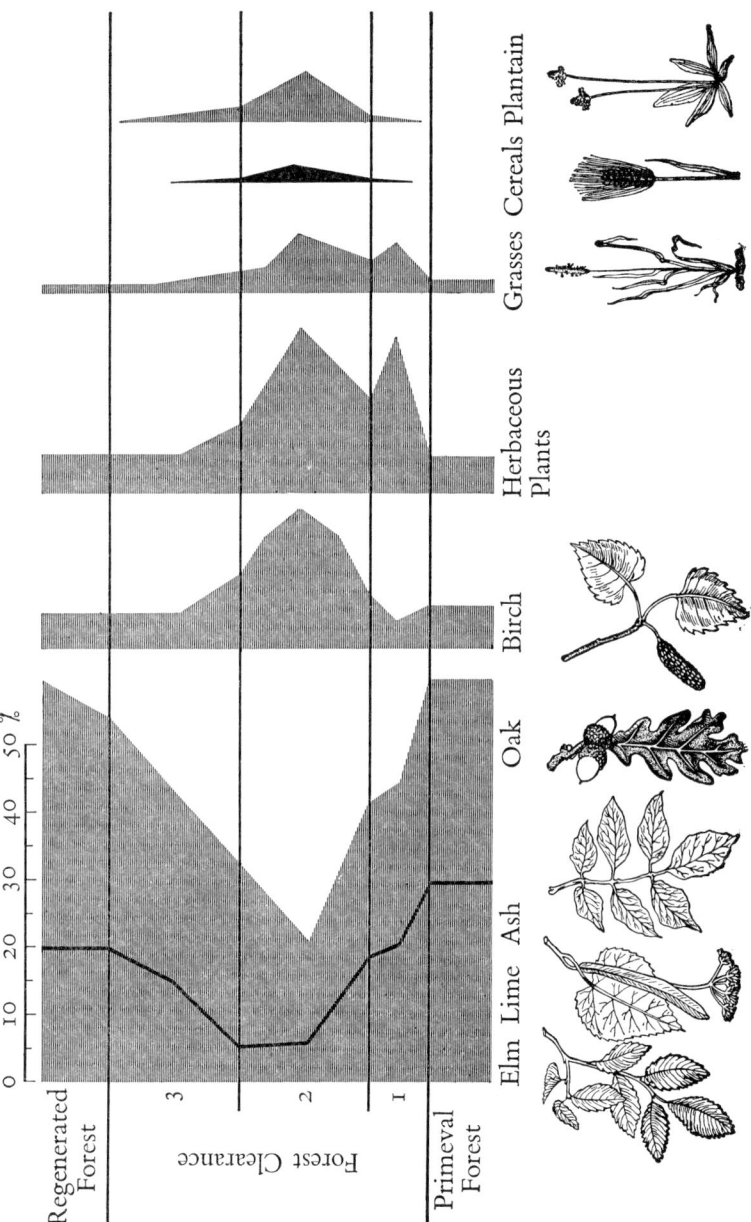

The augite-granophyre rock of Graig Lwyd is very tough and flakes well (Fig. 20*b*). Axe-heads of this material have been found at Windmill Hill in Wiltshire (the earliest Neolithic settlement in Britain), in Somerset in peat dated to 2,600 B.C., and, again, as far north as the Firth of Forth.

The products of the Tievebulliagh factory, made of porcellanite, were traded across the Irish Sea and distributed as far as the London region.

The exact site where the greenstone axe-heads centred in Cornwall were made has not been found, but there is a concentration of them in the Penwith district and it seems probable that the factory was somewhere there. These greenstone axes form the largest group identified and were traded widely.

Small greenstone axe-heads were also made by the Swiss lake-side dwellers, who mounted them in sleeves made of deer-antler; the elasticity of the antler made the wooden haft less likely to split (Fig. 23).

Forest Clearance in Denmark

In northern Europe the effects of forest clearance and the beginnings of agriculture can be traced in pollen diagrams of around 3,000 B.C.

Experiments made recently in Denmark have shown the efficacy of polished stone axe-heads. A genuine Neolithic blade was fitted into an ash-wood shaft, copied from an original haft dating from Neolithic times recovered from Sigerslev Bog (Fig. 25). It was found that the blade broke if fitted too tightly; it had to be left free to vibrate slightly in the haft. The axe was most effective when swung only from the elbow, with short, sharp cuts rather than swinging blows from the shoulder, which is the most effective way of using an axe with a metal blade.

Three men managed to clear 600 square yards of silver birch forest in 4 hours (see Pl. IX). More than 100 trees were felled with one axe-head, which had not been sharpened for about 4,000 years.

Diagrams based on samples of pollen taken by borings in Danish bogs have shown the effects of clearing forests for agricultural purposes about 2,500 B.C. (Fig. 24). As Neolithic farmers cleared large areas of primeval forest, obviously the number of big trees and the quantity of their pollen declined. This is evident in the diagram, from the fall in tree pollen and the rise in the pollen of herbaceous plants (Stage 1 in

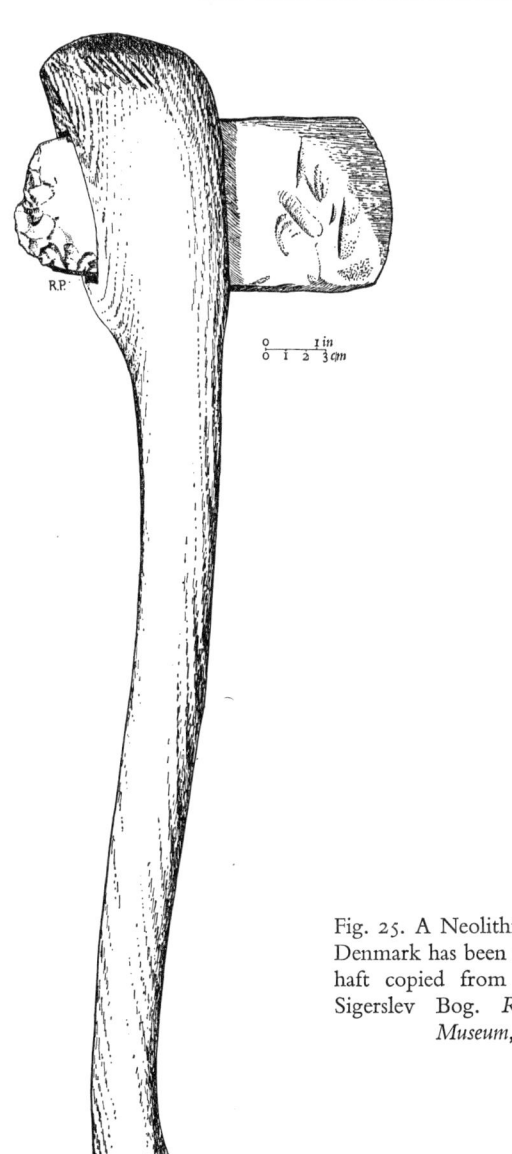

R.P.

0   1 in
0 1 2 3 cm

Fig. 25. A Neolithic chert axe-blade from Denmark has been fitted into an ash-wood haft copied from an original found in Sigerslev Bog. *Restoration by National Museum, Copenhagen.*

Fig. 24). The great increase of birch pollen during Stage 2 suggests that clearings were made largely by burning, for as the seeds of birch require light for germination, the clearance of forest by fire favours the growth of this tree. At the same time the pasture grass pollens increased, and those of cereals and weeds, particularly plantain, *Plantago lanceolata*, suddenly made an appearance—signs that the land, was being used for pasture and cultivation. Finally, the big trees, especially oak, grew up again, indicating that the cultivators had moved on to new territory, presumably because the soil had become exhausted.

5

Transport

Boats

In prehistoric times, as indeed until comparatively recently, travel was mainly by water. Rivers were the arteries of trade; but the fact that people were also well able to cross the sea during the Neolithic stage is attested, for instance, by settlements on Mediterranean islands such as Cyprus, where there was an aceramic village at Khirokitia by 5,690 B.C., and also by the distribution of axe-blades on either side of the Irish Sea.

Before men invented true boats, they must have used floats and rafts which, being perishable, have not survived. The materials doubtless varied from bundles of papyrus, as on the Nile, to wooden logs, as on the Congo, and inflated skins, or hides stretched over frames, as on the Tigris and Euphrates, where there were neither reeds nor trees.

Fig. 26. Stone-age rock engraving of man in skin-covered boat, *Rodoy*, Norway. ⅛. *After J. G. D. Clark.*

Little models of reed rafts, with painted bands to represent the lashing of the bundles, have been attributed to Neolithic and Predynastic times in Egypt. Evidence for the existence of skin-covered boats during the Stone Age of northern Europe is seen in Norwegian rock engravings (Fig. 26). They resembled the *umiak* still used in Arctic waters.

Dug-out canoes could hardly have been common before polished stone axes and adzes came into general use during Neolithic times, though one example, believed to be Mesolithic, was found near Perth

41

and wooden paddles are known from Mesolithic sites in northern Europe. The great solidity of dug-out canoes has ensured their preservation and a number of examples of Neolithic age have been recovered in Scandinavia, Britain, Germany and Switzerland. One group from Aamosen, Denmark, has been dated by pollen analysis to the early part of the Neolithic period (c. 2,500 B.C.). Commonly the canoes were of oak.

The middens of the hunter-fishers of the Neolithic period in Denmark contain bones of deep-sea fish—cod, plaice and dog-fish; this shows that these people certainly had sea-worthy craft, either *umiak* or dug-outs.

Land Vehicles

Sledges were used long before the wheel was invented (see below). The earliest, without runners, were probably made out of hide or bark and could have been dragged equally well over grass, marshes or snow, and to some extent on stony ground. Neolithic men may also have made dug-out sledges in the same way as canoes.

Sledge-runners found in Scandinavian bogs have been dated by pollen-analysis; the earliest are Mesolithic. In some Neolithic examples, the number of uprights supporting the superstructure can be deduced from holes in the runners. These Late Stone Age sledges of northern Europe were probably pulled by dogs or by men on skis; there is no evidence that the reindeer had been domesticated at the time. Remains of skis, the earliest of which are Neolithic, have also been found in Scandinavian bogs.

Wheeled vehicles had a very restricted use in early times owing to the absence of roads. The wheel itself may have been invented first for turning pottery and perhaps applied to converting sledges into carts not long after. Being made of wood, wheels seldom survive; but the potter's wheel leaves characteristic striations on pottery, which is, of course, practically indestructible. In general, the wheel seems to have come into use about 3,000 B.C. in the Middle East. The earliest example of a wooden cart-wheel in Europe is from a Neolithic trackway in the Netherlands. Wheeled vehicles were rare in Europe before the Early Iron Age (500 B.C. onwards).

6

Crafts

A number of new crafts developed during the Neolithic, some of which had been foreshadowed during the Mesolithic and Palaeolithic stages. So long as men depended on hunting and food gathering and were constantly on the move, vessels for the storage of food and drink were made of light, easily portable and usually perishable materials, such as skin and leather bags, baskets, or gourds and ostrich eggshells where these were available. Pottery, being very fragile, was only practicable for people living a fairly static existence and did not come into use before the Neolithic in most areas. The increased security and leisure resulting from the new way of life allowed time for fine craftsmanship and artistry, which was expressed particularly in the manufacture of pottery.

Making vessels in stone also became a fine art in some regions during Neolithic times as a result of improvement in the techniques of pecking and grinding, used also in the production of polished stone axe-heads. The great advantage of stone and pottery over other materials is their ability to withstand heat; this was important now that man had lost the hunter's taste for raw meat and had begun to appreciate the art of cooking. Larger and more durable containers were also necessary for the storage of surplus grain and other foodstuffs which it was now possible to accumulate.

Plant cultivation led to the discovery of spinning and weaving, at first almost exclusively from vegetable fibres, particularly flax. Although spinning is a simple process, weaving requires a loom; this was one of the great inventions made in the Neolithic stage. The production of durable pottery, too, is quite a complicated process and was a most important Neolithic discovery. Just as great pains were taken with the shapes and decorations of pots, so there is evidence of colour and pattern in linen cloth (Pl. XIV*c*). Neolithic crafts were not only utilitarian, but also artistic.

Containers

BASKETRY

Perhaps the earliest known basketry may be represented in the proto-Neolithic level of Shanidar cave, dated to 8,900 B.C. Apart from these examples (which may possibly be matting), the oldest known baskets are those from Çatal Hüyük (6,500 B.C.) which were made from wheat straw. Fine mats from the same level were also preserved in carbonized form as the result of fire. Mud impressions of plain-weave mats have survived at Jarmo, dating from the pre-pottery Neolithic of 6,000 B.C., and at Jericho in the pre-pottery levels there were traces of circular rush mats (Pl. X, in doorway). A potsherd from a site in Kenya known as Gamble's Cave shows clear impressions of basket work; possibly it was a piece from a clay-lined basket which was baked accidentally. The associated Kenya Capsian culture has been dated elsewhere to *c.* 8,600 B.C. and this may be one of the earliest examples of basketry as well as pottery in Africa. By the time of the Fayum lake dwellers, about 4,500 B.C.. the technique of basketry was fully developed, suggesting that it began much earlier. Deep silage pits or granaries at the Fayum sites were lined with coiled corn straw. A boat-shaped basket (Pl. XI*a*) found inside one of these pits may have been used for sowing grain. It is 16 inches long, 10 inches wide, 5½ inches deep, and resembles the work of the Ancient Egyptians of Dynastic times, as well as modern Nubian baskets. It is made in the coiled technique, the earliest and still the most important form of basketry. In this method a core, consisting of a bundle of grass, is coiled spirally; the different layers are then sewn together with a strand of fibre. In the Fayum basket, bast made from flax was used; three coloured vertical strands have been interwoven in the side. A small basket from the Fayum (Pl. XI*b*) has a hollow on the base; such baskets may have been the prototype of Iron Age 'dimple-based' pottery found in East and Central Africa.

LEATHER BAGS

Leather bags were probably made in very early times by drawing a skin over a withy ring and then sewing it in place by thongs threaded through holes pierced with an awl (Pl. XI*d*). Owing to its perishable nature, very few ancient examples of leather are known. Simple bags dating from Dynastic times have been preserved in the dry sand of

Egypt (Pl. XI*c*), and similar vessels are used today in Nubia for carrying water.

Early leather containers are generally extremely hard, resulting from the fact that water was warmed in them by means of heated stones or 'pot-boilers'.

STONE VESSELS

The most important type of stone vessel was the mortar, with its accompanying pestle, an indispensable adjunct to agriculture. Primitive mortars were probably used long before Neolithic times for pounding roots, nuts and also pigments. Characteristic of the Neolithic, however, are the large saddle querns for grinding grain which are found at most early settlements supported by farming (Plate X).

Stone bowls, hollowed out by pecking with a hammerstone and finished by grinding, were also widely used. Fragments of beautifully made bowls, ground until they were smooth as ivory, were found in aceramic levels at Jarmo (Pl. XII*a*). The material used was fine-grained limestone, either uniformly cream in colour or multicoloured on account of veining (Pl. XII*b*). When these stone vessels were superseded by pottery, this veining was sometimes imitated in paint. Possibly the reason why pottery is not found in the earliest Neolithic levels at Jarmo and Jericho was because the art of making stone bowls had reached such perfection locally that alternative material was for long considered unnecessary. At Ali Kosh, Iran, bowls were made out of a variety of materials and some were painstakingly carved out of stone as hard as marble. Possibly they were used to hold gruel made from roasted wheat and barley.

Pottery

At one time, pottery was thought to be one of the essential criteria of Neolithic culture; but later discoveries have shown that it may some-times antedate agriculture and the domestication of animals, for instance in the Sudan and Kenya and also in Denmark. Some of the earliest food-producing communities in the Middle East, as we have seen, did not make pottery at all: the aceramic levels of Jericho, Jarmo and of Hacilar in Anatolia are examples. The earliest known pottery in this part of the world comes from Çatal Hüyük, about 6,800 B.C.

Although some of the first pottery may have resulted from the accidental burning of clay-lined baskets, the manufacture of really satisfactory containers in clay is an intricate process which must have involved a considerable amount of trial and error. The clay must be wet in order to mould it, but the damp pot has to be dried slowly in the sun before baking, for if it is put straight into the fire it will crack. Early attempts often resulted in coarse, fragile pottery because the clay was not well mixed or washed. Gradually, potters learnt to temper the clay, mixing in some grit or vegetable matter to prevent it cracking.

Neolithic potters built up their vessels in spiral coils of clay, or alternatively in successive strips or rings. Before firing, the surface was scraped smooth and afterwards it was often burnished with a pebble or similar rounded object. Sometimes a fine clay 'slip' was applied, which baked hard and smooth. Clay changes colour during firing, mainly according to whether the hot gases in contact with it are oxidizing or reducing in character, but also according to the temperature reached and the composition of the clay. By experimenting with different kinds of clay, and by controlling the air draught and the temperature, potters learnt to produce the desired colour. Black pottery is produced by smothering it so that air is excluded and the gas in contact with the clay is rich in carbon monoxide, a reducing atmosphere. Red pottery is produced by firing in an oxidizing atmosphere.

The potter's wheel came into use only at the time of the metal-using urban civilizations. The oldest surviving example is from Ur, dated 3,250 B.C. It was regularly used in Crete by the beginning of Middle Minoan times, and spread over the Mediterranean by Greek, Etruscan and Punic colonizers. Whereas hand-made pottery is the work of women in primitive societies, the wheel is generally worked by men.

Neolithic pots are almost invariably round-bottomed (Pl. XIII*b*). The shapes and decorations of early pots sometimes resemble their prototypes in leather, basketry, wood or stone (compare Pls. XII and XIII). Pottery made by the earliest Neolithic people in Britain, at Windmill Hill near Avebury, Wiltshire, includes a number of bag-shaped pots reminiscent of leather containers (Pl. XIII*a*). Ornament is confined to lightly incised vertical strokes or a single line of 'pin pricks' just below the rim which may be copied from the holes pierced in leather bags for threading with thongs.

There were a number of regional variants of the Windmill Hill class of pottery, including a large series from a causewayed camp at Abingdon. This 'Abingdon ware' is characterized by thickened, rolled-over rims which seem to imitate leather drawn over a withy ring. There are also lines in the neck of the pot reminiscent of puckered leather (Pl. XIc).

Decorations on pottery resembling basket-work are fairly common; examples are the pots of the 'Gumban A' variant of the Stone Bowl culture of Kenya. The all-over decoration on the outside of these pots evidently imitates a basket; the inside was scratched with deep, irregular lines while the clay was still wet (Fig. 27).

Potsherds are one of the most useful types of artifact from the archaeologist's point of view because they are almost indestructible and relatively small fragments or sherds may be quite distinctive as regards period and culture, either on account of their ornament, texture or form.

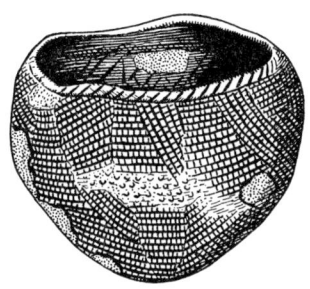

Fig. 27. Pot from Stable's Drift, Kenya. ⅙.
The decoration imitates basket-work. *After*
S. *Cole.*

Spinning and Weaving

In Palaeolithic and Mesolithic times, thread and cord for fastening, binding and sewing must have been made from stalks of grasses and reeds, tree roots or bark fibres, animal sinews and strips of skin. That the early hunting peoples used cords and threads may be inferred from the fact that certain stone and bone artifacts can only have been usable if fastened to handles, probably both by gumming and binding. Bone awls and needles indicate that leather was sewn to form containers or garments. Binding and sewing led to the plaiting of mats and baskets, the making of fishing lines and nets, and the plaiting of cords for carrying heavy objects.

There is no evidence of spinning and weaving before Neolithic times. The chief natural fibres used in these new crafts were bast (vegetable stem fibres), cotton, silk and wool. Wool, being very perishable, has seldom survived from early times and until recently one of the oldest examples was a shroud from an oak dug-out coffin in an Early Bronze Age barrow at Rylstone in Yorkshire. The fire which destroyed the Level VI town at Çatal Hüyük, however, caused the carbonization and preservation of much material, including woollen cloth. These fragments, in fact, are the oldest known textiles (Plate XIVa). Some of the cloth was still clinging to the bones of the dead and at least three different weaves were used. Very probably these people of 6,500 B.C. also made carpets; wall paintings show gay designs not very different from those of modern Anatolian rugs.

Vegetable fibres, particularly flax, were also among the earliest materials spun and woven throughout the Middle East and Egypt; fragments of linen, dating from about 4,500 B.C., were found at Fayum. Cotton was probably made first in India. The oldest cotton fabric is from Mohenjodaro, dating from the Early Bronze Age (c. 2,500 B.C.), but as the thread is far from being of primitive uncultivated type it appears likely that development from the wild plant had been effected in the preceding period.

Spinning consists of drawing out and twisting the fibres into thread. At first this was done by hand, the thread being wound on to a stick. From this developed the idea of a spindle, consisting of a tapered stick weighted with a whorl (Pl. XIVb). A length of fibre was fastened to the spindle either by being caught under a hook in the stem, or wound round a groove. The fibres are paid out while the spindle is rotated by hand, dropped and allowed to swing. The whorl acts as a weight to maintain the spin, producing a fine, even thread. Spindle-whorls (Fig. 28a) made of stone, clay or bone are found at many Neolithic sites in the Middle East, Egypt and Europe and provide the evidence for spinning.

Any apparatus for stretching the warp may be called a loom. The simplest method of weaving is by the horizontal ground loom, which is depicted pictorially in Egypt from about 4,000 B.C.—for instance, on the inside of a dish from Badari (Fig. 28b). The horizontal loom is still used by nomadic people of the Middle East. Vertical looms were

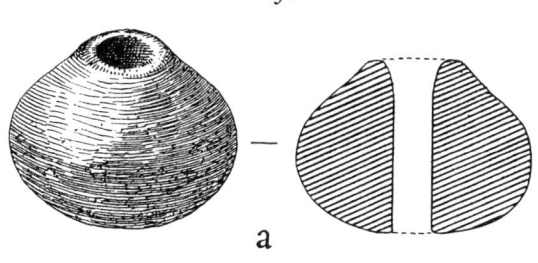

a

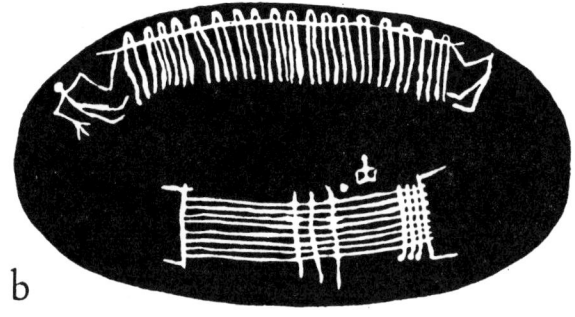

b

Fig. 28. (a) Baked clay spindle-whorl. Neolithic lake-side village, Switzerland. ¾.
(b) Horizontal ground loom depicted on the inside of a pottery dish from Badari,
Egypt, *c.* 4,400 B.C. ⅓. *After Crowfoot.*

an improvement and came into use somewhat later. Evidence of
weaving at many Neolithic sites comes from loom weights. Such
weights, of stone or clay, were pierced with holes and each was tied
to a bundle of warp threads.

All textiles before about 2,500 B.C. were in plain weave, in which a
series of wefts passes over and under a series of warps, as in darning.
Fragments of linen found at the Fayum show that the weave was
fairly even; the thread used was so lightly spun that it is difficult to
see a twist. Whereas cotton and wool have only to be cleansed and
teased out, bast fibres must be soaked (retted), beaten, scraped and
combed out before spinning; the fact that linen from the Fayum has
been preserved for over 6,000 years shows that these processes must
have been well understood by the Neolithic craftsmen.

Abundant examples of burnt flax yarn and pieces of linen in the

Swiss lake-side villages, as well as numerous clay spindle whorls and
loom weights, provide evidence that weaving was an important occupation in these Neolithic communities. A fragment of textile found
at Irgenhausen (Pl. XIV*c*) shows that the complicated technique of
brocading to produce a pattern standing out from the ground was
already well developed.

Although weaving was practised by the continental forerunners of
the Neolithic settlers in Britain, there is no evidence of it before Bronze
Age times in this country. The clothing of the Neolithic inhabitants
of Britain was probably mainly of goatskin or sheepskin.

Art : Domestic and Religious

Neolithic people are not renowned for their pictorial art; they produced little in any way comparable to the magnificent cave paintings
of late Palaeolithic times. Their creative energies seem to have been
expended rather in the building of vast and elaborate tombs (described
in the next chapter) and, to a certain extent, in the decoration of
pottery. There are some examples of fine sculpture, but they are very
rare.

Hunters, as would be expected, were interested almost exclusively
in the animals upon which they depended for their food supply and the
finest paintings of Palaeolithic times show mammoth, bison, deer, wild
cattle and horses. Neolithic farmers, on the other hand, were concerned with the production of crops and breeding of animals and
consequently fertility and increase were of the utmost importance.
Hence there arose among them the concept of 'mother earth' and the
cult of a 'mother goddess'. Female figurines or 'Venuses' were carved
during late Palaeolithic times, but they were presumably associated
with human fertility rather than with the idea of the earth itself as the
mother of all life. That the latter idea prevailed in Neolithic times is
borne out by the beliefs of those primitive peoples of the present day
who are dependent on the soil for their livelihood, particularly where
women are the cultivators.

A site which has completely revolutionized our knowledge of the
religious beliefs and artistic products of Neolithic peoples is Çatal
Hüyük, excavated only since 1961. By 1965, about forty shrines had
been uncovered in the various levels. In many of these the fertility

goddess, modelled in plaster, is associated with bulls, rams and human breasts, symbols of birth and the continuity of life. Such symbols nearly always appear on the west walls; but on the east walls, below which the dead were buried, there are symbols of death in the form of wall paintings of vultures and the jaws of such scavengers as pigs, foxes and weasels.

Most fascinating of all in view of its tremendous development in later times is the bull cult at Çatal Hüyük, unique for this period. Plastered bulls' heads appear beside the goddess or between her upraised legs and sometimes there is a combination of a bull's horns and a modelled human breast. In one shrine in Level VI, a plaster goddess nearly 4 feet high is shown giving birth to a huge bull's head and facing her are three bulls' heads above two rows of breasts. The bulls' heads were originally painted with red muzzles and hand impressions on the nose, suggesting that participants in the fertility ceremonies touched the animals' faces with hands smeared in red ochre.

In the earlier levels the bulls' horns, like their heads, were modelled in plaster; but from the time of Level VI onwards, the actual horns were incorporated (the horns have perished, but the horn-cores remain). Often the horns were built into mud-brick pillars; from their position, it seems that their purpose was to protect the platform which was used for sleeping and beneath which the dead were buried.

Vultures, symbolizing death, were depicted in a spectacular series of wall paintings. Sometimes they are shown with human legs, hovering over headless human corpses. Mr. James Mellaart, the excavator of this remarkable site, suggests that the birds with human legs may represent priests disguised for the performance of burial rites.

Other wall paintings show hunting scenes, with men wearing leopard skins pursuing wild bulls, boars, bears, stags, onagers and other animals. Often the men are touching the animal's tail or tongue, probably representing man's control over them. Leopards were evidently held in high esteem and are often associated with the goddess in her role of 'mistress of animals'. In a shrine in Level VI a pair of leopards, probably a male and a female, were modelled in clay mixed with straw and had been painted over at least 40 times, probably once a year at special ceremonies. The paint was carefully peeled off, layer by layer, and revealed different designs; the later animals were yellow with black spots and pink claws, mouth and tip of tail, whereas the earlier ones were white, with black and white rosettes and red claws. In an earlier 'leopard shrine' in Level VII, the later leopards were decorated with crosses while the earlier ones had rosettes. Yet another pair of leopards was discovered in 1965 in Level X; the animals have their tails up, as though fighting.

Several stone figurines from Çatal Hüyük show both men and women associated with leopards. Most beautiful of all the figurines, perhaps, is one in clay showing a woman giving birth to a child, seated on a throne with felines on either side (in this case no spots are shown and it is possible that the animals may be lions rather than leopards). This figurine was found in a grain bin, where it was presumably placed to increase the fertility of the crops.

These figurines are presumably ancestral to the amazing clay statuettes discovered at Hacilar, also in Turkey, in 1960. They date from about 5,500 B.C. and depict the fertility goddess in a great number of attitudes, sometimes seated on a leopard. These 40 or so statuettes are among the finest and most imaginative examples of Neolithic art known. Other figurines of considerable artistic merit are those from a tomb in eastern Rumania associated with the Hamangia culture (its middle phase has been dated by radiocarbon to about 3,600 B.C.). One of these figurines represents a woman, the other a man supporting his head with his hands as though lost in thought (Plate XV). Figures of men are much rarer than those of women and this one is most unusual in his attitude. Also curious is a hermaphrodite 'god-dolly' associated with a Neolithic track in the Somerset fens. It is made of ash wood and a radiocarbon date of about 2,900 B.C. was obtained from timber overlying the track. One theory is that the figure was a votive offering, left to ensure success in the building of a new track.

No parallels for the cults of Çatal Hüyük are known from other Neolithic sites, where almost the only evidence of religious beliefs comes from figurines. The haunting figures carved by pre-Neolithic fishermen on river boulders at Lepenski Vir, near the Iron Gates of the Danube, are also unique. The human faces have an extraordinary variety of expressions—serene or stern, or sometimes anguished, with wide, staring eyes and full grimacing lips. We can only speculate on their purpose, but their position round hearths in the centre of the houses suggests that they were connected with some ritual.

Occasionally, collections of human skulls suggesting ancestor worship have been found, such as a number of restored human heads under the floor of a house dating from the pre-pottery period at

Jericho (Plate XVIII). They had been modelled with such care that it may be supposed that they represented venerated members of the family. The features below the temples of these portrait heads were modelled in plaster on the actual bones of the face, the tops of the skulls being left bare except for traces of paint on some of them. On one of the restored faces there are indications in paint of a moustache. The eyes are represented by inset pieces of shell.

7

Buildings

Villages and Houses

The earliest Neolithic settlements were evidently situated on hill slopes above the 'fertile crescent' of western Asia, and on the uplands of Anatolia, where sufficient rainfall allowed the growth of wild wheat and barley; or by springs at lower levels. It was not until much later that communities moved to the flood plains of the great rivers of Iraq.

On present evidence, by far the most ancient town (for it was more than a village) was built at Tell es-Sultan, Jericho. The site is exceptional, being an oasis 840 feet below sea-level fed by a perennial spring, which was already frequented by Natufian food-gatherers soon after 8,000 B.C. A long period of increasingly permanent occupation followed. It is provisionally estimated that by 7,500 B.C. the site had become a proto-Neolithic village, and within 700 years had acquired the character of a town. The mound or 'tell' which now occupies the site is composed entirely of the debris of human occupation accumulated over thousands of years. Excavation has shown that a mound 45 feet high had grown from the ruins of successive superimposed buildings even before the first pottery appeared (Fig. 29).

Two main building stages have been identified during the pre-pottery Neolithic at Jericho. The earliest recognizable houses, dating

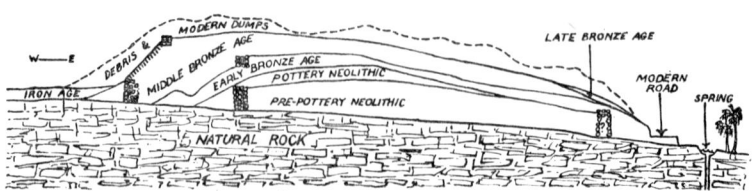

Fig. 29. Section through mound at Jericho composed of the debris of human occupation accumulated from about 8,000 B.C. to the present time. Height of mound *c.* 100 feet. *After M. Wheeler.*

from about 6,800 B.C., were made of mud bricks, lens-shaped in section, which have been called 'hog-backed bricks'. The houses were round in plan and their walls inclined inwards, suggesting that they were once domed. Perhaps the roofs were made of plastered branches, as there are many traces of timber and wattle in the walls; the floors were of beaten mud.

The houses of the second pre-pottery phase were rectangular in plan, built of thumb-impressed bricks, and with well-burnished plaster floors and walls. This second pre-pottery phase has been dated by the radio carbon method to about 6,250 B.C.

Five successive town walls were constructed during the pre-pottery period (Plate XVI). They were built of undressed but regularly arranged stones. The third wall, associated with the 'hog-backed brick' phase, is by far the most imposing. It was backed by at least one solid stone tower 40 feet in diameter, and still surviving to a height of 30 feet, with a stairway descending through the middle of it and leading into a passage. In front of the tower lay a ditch 28 feet wide and 8 feet deep cut out of the solid limestone. The inhabitants, in fact, took no chances as far as defence was concerned. It has been suggested that the 'hog-backed brick' people were defending themselves against the 'plaster floor' people who eventually succeeded them.

After the pre-pottery period there was a sharp break and the site was then occupied by the first pottery users, who apparently built no permanent structures. They were succeeded by another group who made different pottery and who built houses of bun-shaped bricks, inferior to those of the pre-pottery people.

During its pre-pottery phases the Neolithic town of Jericho must have occupied some 8 to 10 acres and may have had a population approaching 2,000 people.

The largest Neolithic settlement known is Çatal Hüyük, covering 32 acres and four times as big as pre-pottery Jericho. It was a flourishing town by 6,800 B.C. (Level XII) and nobody knows how long before that, since the excavations have not yet reached bedrock. Its wealth was founded on agriculture and trade. Access to the rooms must have been by means of a wooden ladder from the courts on to the flat roof and thence via a shaft and finally head-first through a low doorway; presumably this inconvenient method was necessary for purposes of defence. The living rooms had built-in furniture consisting of benches and platforms, as well as hearths and ovens, all made of

earth and plaster. Groups of rooms, each with a storeroom, were centred round shrines. A remarkable wall painting from a shrine in Level
VII shows what is probably a view of the town with a volcano erupting
in the background, probably the mountain of Hasan Dag from where
the inhabitants obtained obsidian, an important article of trade.

Whereas Çatal Hüyük and Jericho were towns or cities, Qalat Jarmo
was a village. The mound lies at 2,600 feet above sea-level in the hills
east of modern Kirkuk in Iraq; it covers three acres and is built up of
25 feet of occupation debris. The village was perhaps founded soon
after 7,000 B.C.; radiocarbon dates ranging from more than 6,000 B.C.
have been obtained for the pre-pottery phase at Jarmo and the foundations must have been earlier still.

Associated with Neolithic culture at Jarmo there are some twelve
different building stages, pottery appearing only in the upper third of
this sequence. The earliest houses were rectilinear, built of packed mud
or *pisé*. Sometimes the walls had stone foundations. Many of the houses
contained ovens and basins baked into the floors (Plate XVII).

At Tepe Guran in Luristan, Iran, there was a semi-permanent village
with wooden houses about 6,500 B.C. By 5,800 B.C. it was replaced by a
permanent village of brick-walled houses. Pre-Neolithic peoples too
lived in settlements which continued to exist over long periods. During
the earlier periods at Lepenski Vir, Yugoslavia, they lived in unique
trapeze-shaped houses which followed the shape of the steep recess
which enclosed the settlement on the right bank of the Danube. Post-
holes indicate that the houses were made of wood. During the third
period, around 5,000 B.C. and by now fully Neolithic, the old architec-
tural plan was abandoned and the settlement spread out of the recess
and along the river bank.

Different ecological conditions naturally influenced building
materials. In the Middle East and in south-eastern Europe, the climate
was dry enough to allow buildings with mud walls. At Karanova in
Bulgaria, for instance, a sequence of five settlements was found with
houses having *pisé* walls over 1 foot thick. West of the point where the
river Tisza joins the Danube, in the damper temperate forest zone,
timber was plentiful and was used almost everywhere for building. A
wet climate necessitates a good run-off by means of a sloping roof,
with eaves sloping from a ridge-pole supported by a line of posts. The
walls consisted of other posts interwoven with wattle or of split saplings
plastered with dung or clay. The earliest houses of the fifth millennium

B.C. in the region of the lower Danube, were rectangular with walls of split tree trunks filled in with wattle and daub; the houses contained a front porch and a central fireplace.

In 1967 a rectangular house, 7 × 6 m. and walled on two sides with thin split planks of oak, was found at Ballynagilly, Co. Tyrone in Northern Ireland. Associated pottery suggests a date of about 3,000 B.C. The resemblance between this planked house and those of central Europe supports the hypothesis, based on pottery styles, that the Neolithic colonizers of Ulster came from central Europe by way of northern England rather than from Spain and western France.

In the loess country of central Europe, three basic types of house were built. The earliest and most imposing were long timber buildings up to 100 feet in length. Rather later came smaller-two-roomed houses like those of the lower Danube. Finally, still smaller dwellings were built, with a single chamber.

Among the best preserved examples of the early 'long houses' are those of the village of Köln Lindental, south-west of Cologne, which had an estimated population of up to 300. In these houses the walls were built partly of split timbers and partly of wattle and daub and the ridge-pole was supported by posts set at intervals in three parallel rows. There were separate store-houses, possibly for stocks of seed-grain, grouped inside a ditch and bank recalling the 'causewayed camps' of the first Neolithic settlers in Britain, such as Windmill Hill.

The second type of house, with two rooms, is represented in the lake-side villages of Switzerland; the wooden parts were preserved wherever they became water-logged by a rise in the lake-level or by subsidence. At Aichbühl on the Federsee in Württemberg (Fig. 30), the houses rested on a framework of beams laid over soft ground. At some sites, perhaps where there was danger of flooding, the houses were raised a few feet above the ground. At one time the houses were thought to have been built on piles in the lake itself, but this view is no longer held. Many of the houses had thick floors of packed clay to keep out the damp. The inner room contained supports for a couch, with a hearth against the partition; food was evidently prepared in the outer room, where there were clay ovens. In front of the houses there was often a planked forecourt.

During the late Neolithic phase in central Europe, the houses were much simpler, perhaps owing to the fact that more emphasis was laid on pastoralism than on cultivation. At Goldberg in Württemberg, for

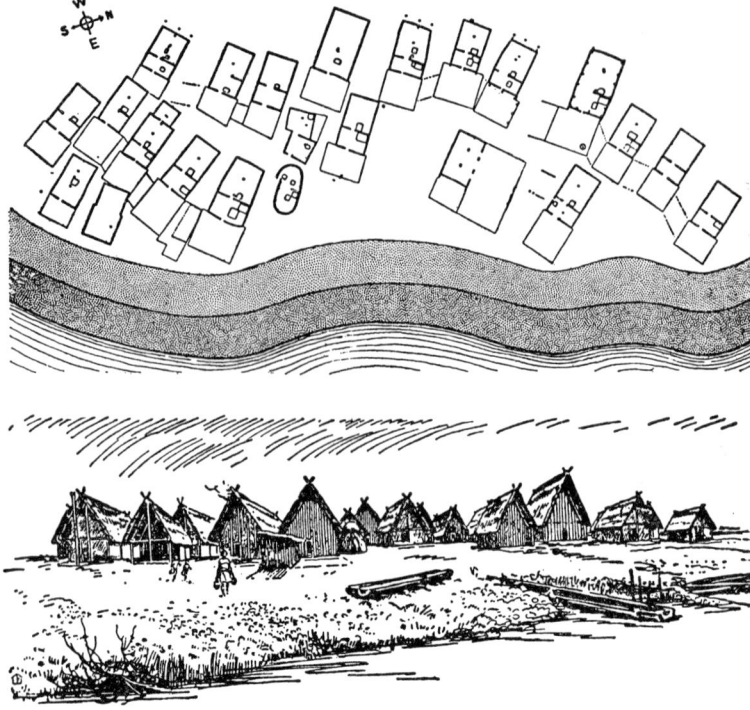

Fig. 30. Plan and reconstruction of Neolithic lake-side village, Aichbühl, Württemberg. *After Schmidt.*

instance, the huts of this period were only about 14 feet square. They contained a large central pit (perhaps a storage silo) and a hearth in the sunken floor. The walls were made of thin saplings.

Excavations of Neolithic settlements in Denmark have revealed indications of long rectangular houses divided into small rooms, each of which probably held a single family. One of two such houses comprising the settlement at Barkaer was 266 feet long, and was divided into twenty-six rooms. The walls were probably of wattle and daub; the roof was carried by a number of posts in stone-lined sockets.

Exceptions to the timber houses of Neolithic Europe are found in outlying places where wood was scarce, such as Skara Brae in the Orkneys. Here not only the buildings were of stone, but also the furniture; beds, for instance, were constructed of stone slabs.

Tombs

Generally speaking, there is little evidence that Palaeolithic peoples were much concerned with an after-life, although Mousterian and Upper Palaeolithic hunters occasionally buried their dead with ceremony, particularly in caves. The oldest known cemeteries are Mesolithic. Nomads seldom take much trouble over the burial of the dead; but as soon as people began to live in settled communities, the dead were usually interred in carefully made graves, sometimes grouped in cemeteries, occasionally dug near the dwelling place. Food and drink tools and weapons—'grave goods'—were placed with the bodies during the later part of the Neolithic and in the Early Bronze Age.

The megalith builders brought tomb construction to a fine art. From the Mediterranean they spread northwards up the Atlantic coast leaving monumental standing stones, stone circles and graves to mark their passage. Recent radiocarbon dates show that they reached Iberia by about 3,500 B.C. and Brittany by 3,200 B.C.

The graves of the earliest Neolithic settlers in Britain, associated with 'causewayed camps', are the so-called long barrows (Fig. 31*a*). The largest and most characteristic, up to 300 feet long and 15 feet high,

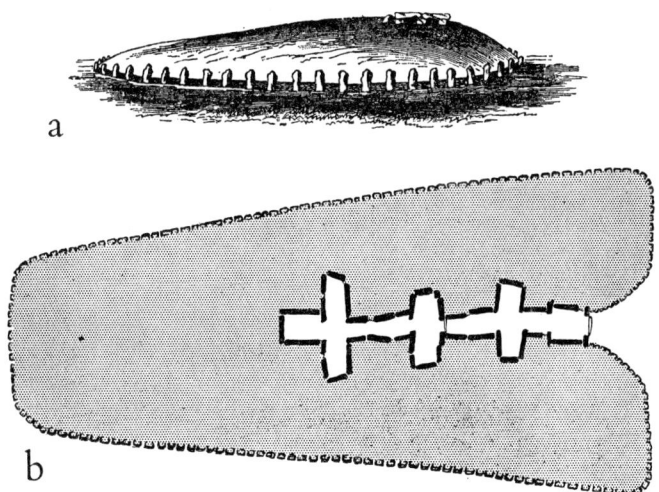

Fig. 31. (a) Reconstruction of long barrow. *After Thurnam.* (b) Plan of long barrow, Stoney Littleton, Somerset. Length *c.* 100 ft. *After Piggott.*

are in Wiltshire, Dorset and the Cotswolds. The mounds were built up of material excavated from flanking ditches. Collective burials were grouped at one end, within internal structures of wood, turf or stone; or they were placed in cells opening off the sides of a central gallery (Fig. 31*b*). Antler from the Windmill Hill long barrow has been dated recently by radiocarbon to about 3,200 B.C.

A barrow 50 m. long at Ascott-under-Wychwood, Oxfordshire, is particularly important because there is evidence of Neolithic occupation of up to 500 years before the barrow was built (and Mesolithic below that). The mound was built by piling earth on either side of a central spine of stones and hurdles, the latter represented by rows of stake holes. The central area between the spine and the walls was in places divided off by partitions and the plan as a whole is similar to that of Continental Neolithic houses. At least 20 people were buried in the barrow, but only parts of their skeletons were present.

There were two main classes of chambered tombs, namely *gallery graves* in which the entrance opens immediately into an elongated rectangular chamber; and *passage graves* in which there are two distinct elements—the burial chamber or chambers and the approach passage. Gallery graves are usually under long cairns (or long barrows), passage graves generally under circular cairns. The latter type, dating mainly from the transition Neolithic to Early Bronze Age, is particularly characteristic of the Boyne Valley in Ireland (e.g. New Grange), but there is a well-preserved outlying example of this type at Bryn Celli Ddu in Anglesey. The polygonal burial chamber, roofed with capstones, is approached by a passage leading from a roofed portal. The whole was covered by a round cairn 90 feet in diameter and 12 feet high. Passage graves under stone mounds (*dysser*) are also common in Denmark, where they date from the end of the Early and the Middle Neolithic stages.

The construction of artificial hills for 'houses of the dead' is believed to have been derived originally from the use of caves in natural hills as burial places. The internal structures of long barrows and chambered tombs may have reflected to some extent domestic architecture of the period.

Neolithic villages in the Middle East do not appear to have had cemeteries or elaborate tombs comparable with those of western Europe. In Early Jericho, for instance, the dead were buried under the floors of the houses, with the heads buried separately; and at Çatal

Hüyük the corpses were placed beneath the sleeping platforms after removal of the flesh.

Sanctuaries

It is a remarkable fact that the spring at Jericho, which became the site of the oldest known town, appears to have been revered from very early times. On bed-rock below the accumulated debris of Neolithic and later civilizations, Natufian implements are associated with traces of a structure dating from about 7,800 B.C., with sockets for massive poles, possibly totem poles, which suggest that it was a sanctuary. Dr. Kathleen Kenyon considers that Natufian hunters were accustomed to visit the spring and, recognizing its vital importance, established a holy place beside it.

At Beidha, Jordan, three curious buildings outside the village are believed to be associated with some kind of religious observance. They contained several large slabs of sandstone and a huge, shallow sandstone basin. There was also a layer of some kind of iron compound, foreign to the region and therefore brought in and laid there on purpose.

The shrines of Çatal Hüyük (Fig. 32) are identical with the living rooms apart from the amazing plaster reliefs and sculptures of bulls and goddesses already described. The rites performed in them, undoubtedly concerned mainly with fertility, seem to form a link with the Upper Palaeolithic on the one hand and with the Bronze Age on the other, probably foreshadowing the bull cult of Minoan Crete. Other early sanctuaries were associated with burial grounds, for example the construction with rock-basins adjoining the late Mesolithic cemetery at Mugharet-el-Wad in Palestine.

At Lepenski Vir, Yugoslavia, the hearth formed the centre of each house, which was evidently used for magic rites as well as for living and working. The hearths are in the form of a sunken basin lined with stone blocks and surrounded by slabs. They are outlined by an ornamental frieze of thin red stone slabs set vertically into the floor and forming triangles. Most remarkable of all are the sculptures (p. 52) which stood near the hearths.

The earliest of the temples in Malta, such as those of Skorba which were excavated in 1961–62, as well as the oldest part of Stonehenge (dating from about 2,000 B.C.), were the work of Neolithic communities. This 'Stonehenge I' comprises a circular ditch with inner

Fig. 32. Reconstruction of part of the First Shrine, Level VI, Çatal Hüyük. On the north wall is a plaster figure of a bull 8 ft. long. On the east wall are three bulls' heads above two rows of modelled women's breasts. *After J. Mellaart.*

bank surrounding a ring of pits (the 'Aubrey Holes'), many of which contained cremated burials. Also dating from this phase is the large, bluntly pointed sarsen-stone (the Heel Stone), possibly of phallic significance, which stands outside the circular enclosure, on the north-east side close to the entrance causeway. Post-holes near the Heel Stone, and rows of post-holes on the causeway, are believed to have held uprights of timber structures.

To the Neolithic people the world of spirits or deities was mainly a nether-world, that is to say essentially *of the earth*; but with the coming of the Bronze Age the idea of sky-gods appears to have developed. The stone circles which constitute Stonehenge II and III were built by the bearers of Bronze Age culture, whose religious interests were evidently centred on the sun, for these structures were aligned approximately on the midsummer sunrise. Professor Gerald Hawkins put forward the theory that Stonehenge was an elaborate astronomical observatory and Professor Fred Hoyle goes even further suggesting that the Aubrey Holes formed a protractor.

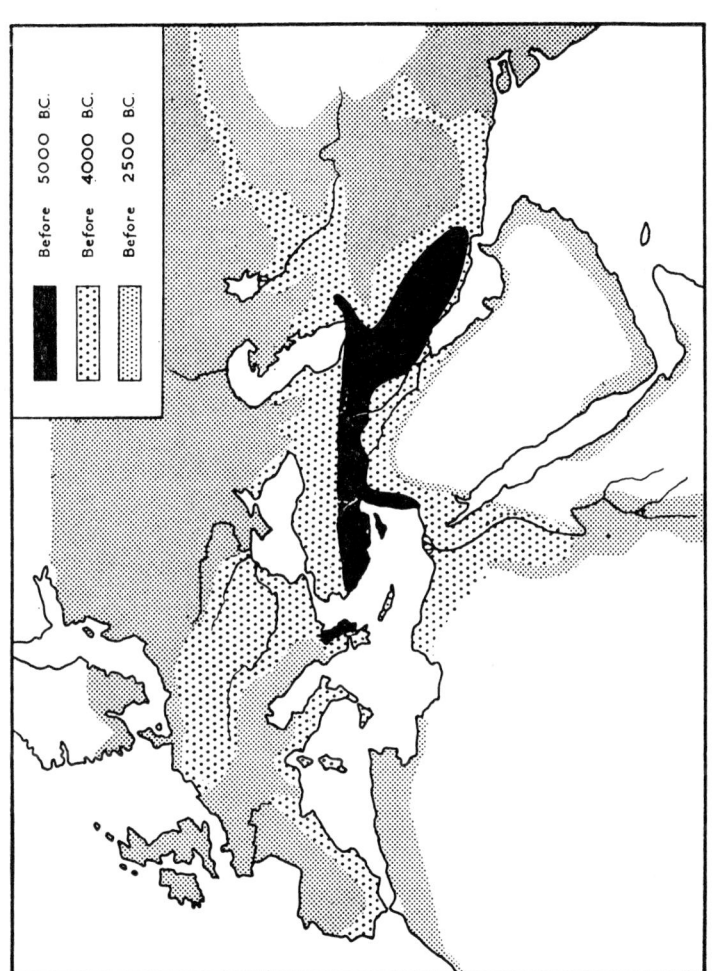

Fig. 33. The spread of Neolithic culture from its origins in the Middle East, *c.* 8,000 B.C. to dawn of the Bronze Age in Europe, *c.* 2,000 B.C.

Before 5000 BC.

Before 4000 BC.

Before 2500 BC.

Summary

Food-producing, hallmark of the stage known as the Neolithic, began to supplement food-gathering in the Middle East at least by 8,000 B.C. The principal plants cultivated were cereals (wheat and barley), pulses, flax and fruit. While the Neolithic economy of the Middle East and Europe was based on the cultivation of wheat, the most important crops in the Far East were rice and millet and, in Central America, maize.

The wild ancestors of domestic goats and sheep lived in the areas of the Middle East where wheat and barley also grew wild; the beginnings of agriculture and animal husbandry, therefore, took place in the same region. Hunting and fishing continued, sometimes with the aid of new devices, but became less important as food supplies became assured through farming. A more settled mode of life was now possible and specialized craftsmen and traders could be supported.

Neolithic people constructed permanent dwellings, sometimes within fortified villages and even towns. Their activities included the systematic mining of flint and obsidian, the manufacture and trading of polished stone axe-heads and their use in clearing forest for agriculture. New crafts were also developed, such as basketry, the making of stone vessels and pottery, and spinning and weaving.

According to recent radiocarbon dating, the earliest Neolithic towns and villages in the Near and Middle East, such as Çatal Hüyük, Jericho I and Jarmo, were approximately contemporary with early Mesolithic hunter-fisher camps in Europe, for instance Star Carr in Yorkshire, dating from about 7,000 B.C. Except in naturally irrigated areas around springs (e.g. Jericho) or on flood-plains (e.g. the Nile Valley), Neolithic farmers using simple 'slash-and-burn' methods of cultivation frequently needed to move to new tracts of land as the soil on the old became exhausted. Thus, with expansion of the population, Neolithic culture soon spread from its nuclear areas in the Middle East and the Mediterranean basin up the Danube valley, over much of the lowlands of Germany and as far as the Middle Elbe before 4,000 B.C. (Fig. 33). A thousand years later it had reached the shores of the Atlantic, the British Isles and southern Scandinavia. The first farmers were apparently peaceful, but warring groups appeared in parts of Europe towards the end of Neolithic and early Bronze Age times, such as the warrior pastoralists who brought the Battle-axe culture into western Europe about 1,900 B.C.

The term Neolithic implies a certain stage of culture, not an absolute period of time. The earliest Neolithic of the Middle East was contemporary with Mesolithic Europe; the later Neolithic of north-west Europe existed at the same time as the Bronze Age urban civilizations of the Middle East. The Neolithic stage lasted from about 7,500 B.C. to 3,000 B.C. in the Middle East, from 3,000 B.C. to 1,800 B.C. in Britain. The Polynesians were still in a Neolithic stage of culture when they reached New Zealand about 1,000 A.D., and so they remained until recent years.

In Britain, the Neolithic began with the arrival of farmer immigrants, but these newcomers did not replace the Mesolithic hunter-fishers, who for some time continued their way of life much as before and only gradually assimilated the elements of Neolithic economy. It was thus that the so-called Secondary Neolithic cultures arose, represented for instance by the chipped flint axes known as Thames picks, and by settlements such as those in the Orkneys, at Skara Brae. The stone axe factories also seem to have been worked by people of Secondary Neolithic culture.

In every stage of culture there is a characteristic division of labour. On the analogy of recent societies on a similar technological level, it is inferred that Neolithic activities such as spinning and weaving, hoe cultivation (without the plough) and pottery making (without the wheel) were the tasks of women; men's work included herding, mining, axe-making, tree-felling and building.

Artistic expression seldom if ever reached the heights of the Palaeolithic cave paintings and Neolithic people were non-literate, writing having been invented only during the Bronze Age. Their religion appears to have been founded on worship of the Earth mother goddess, symbolizing fertility. Probably the greatest achievements of a non-utilitarian nature in Neolithic culture were the lavish decoration of pottery, construction of elaborate tombs, figurines, and, at Çatal Hüyük, amazing wall paintings and plaster reliefs. The idea of building megalithic stone tombs under mounds or cairns originated in the Mediterranean region with the beginnings of Bronze Age civilization, before 3,000 B.C., and was adopted by Neolithic people in western and north-western Europe.

References

ANDERSON, E. 1952. *Plants, Man and Life.* viii+245 pp., 16 text-figs. Boston, Mass.

ANGRESS, S. & REED, C. A. 1962. An annotated bibliography on the origin and descent of domestic mammals 1900–1955. *Fieldiana: Anthropology*, vol. 54, no. 1. Chicago Natural History Museum.

ANON. 1968. Neolithic house in Ulster. *Nature*, vol. 220, p. 422.

ARKELL, A. J. 1953. *Shaheinab.* xix+114 pp., 43 pls., 57 text-figs. Oxford.

ASHBEE, P. & SMITH, I. 1966. The date of the Windmill Hill Long Barrow. *Antiquity*, vol. 40, p. 299.

ATKINSON, R. J. C. 1956. *Stonehenge.* 210 pp., 25 pls., 8 text-figs. London.

BERCIU, D. 1960. Neolithic Figurines from Rumania. *Antiquity*, vol. 34, p. 283.

BILTON, L. 1957. The Chillingham Herd of Wild Cattle. *Trans. Nat. Hist. Soc., Northumberland, Durham, Newcastle*, vol. 12, no. 5.

BRAIDWOOD, R. J. 1957. *Prehistoric Men.* 3rd ed., 187 pp., 50 figs. Chicago Natural History Museum.

BRAIDWOOD, R. J. 1958. Near Eastern Prehistory. *Science*, vol. 127, pp. 1419–1430.

BRAIDWOOD, R. J. *et al.* 1960. *Prehistoric Investigations in Iraqi Kurdistan.* Oriental Institute University of Chicago Studies in Ancient Oriental Civilization, No. 31. Chicago.

BRAIDWOOD, R. J. & REED, C. A. 1957. The Achievement and Early Consequences of Food-Production: A Consideration of the Archaeological and Natural-Historical Evidence. *Cold Spring Harbor Symposia on Quantitative Biology*, vol. 22, pp. 19–31.

BRAILSFORD, J. W. 1953. *Later Prehistoric Antiquities of the British Isles.* x+81 pp., 23 pls., 26 text-figs. British Museum, London.

BRYUSOV, A. 1956. Neolithic Dwellings in the Forest Zone of the European Part of the U.S.S.R. *Proc. Prehist. Soc.*, vol. 21 (1955), pp. 77–83.

CHILDE, V. G. 1936. *Man Makes Himself.* xii+275 pp., 11 text-figs. London.

CHILDE, V. G. 1947. *Prehistoric Communities of the British Isles.* 2nd ed. xiv+274 pp., 16 pls., 96 text-figs. London.

CHILDE, V. G. 1953. Old World Prehistory: Neolithic. *In* A. L. Kroeber, *Anthropology Today*, Chicago, pp. 193–210.

CHILDE, V. G. 1957. *The Dawn of European Civilization.* 6th ed. xiii+368 pp. London.

CHILDE, V. G. 1958. *The Prehistory of European Society.* 185 pp., 2 maps. London.

CLARK, J. G. D. 1945. Farmers and Forests in Neolithic Europe. *Antiquity*, vol. 19, pp. 57–71.

CLARK, J. G. D. 1952. *Prehistoric Europe: The Economic Basis.* xvii + 349 pp., 16 pls., 180 text-figs. London.

CLARK, J. G. D. 1965. Radiocarbon Dating and the Spread of Farming Economy. *Antiquity*, vol. 39, pp. 45–48.

CLARK, J. G. D. & GODWIN, H. 1962. The Neolithic in the Cambridgeshire Fens. *Antiquity*, vol. 36, pp. 10–23.

CLARK, J. G. D. & PIGGOTT, S. 1965. *Prehistoric Societies.* 356 pp., 8 pls., 95 text figs., 4 maps. London.

CLUTTON-BROCK, J. 1962. Near Eastern Canids and the Affinities of the Natufian Dogs. *Zeitschrift für Tierzüchtung und Züchtungsbiologie*, vol. 76, pp. 325–333.

CLUTTON-BROCK, J. 1963. The Origins of the Dog. *Science in Archaeology* (eds. D. Brothwell & E. Higgs), London, pp. 269–73.

COLES, J. 1968. A Neolithic god-dolly from Somerset, England. *Antiquity*, vol. 42, pp. 275–277.

CROWFOOT, G. M. 1954. Textiles, Basketry and Mats. *In* C. Singer *et alia, A History of Technology*, Oxford, vol. 1, pp. 413–447.

CURWEN, E. C. 1946. *Plough and Pasture.* viii + 122 pp., 14 pls., 21 text-figs. London.

DEGERBOL, M. 1961. On a find of a Preboreal domestic dog from Star Carr, Yorkshire. *Proceedings of the Prehistoric Society*, vol. 27, p. 35.

EVANS, J. D. 1964. Excavations in the Neolithic mound of Knossos 1958–60. *Bulletin of the Institute of Archaeology*, No. 4, pp. 35–60.

GUYAN, W. U. *et alia.* 1955. Das Pfahlbauproblem. *Monographien zur Ur- und Frühgeschichte der Schweiz*, Bd. 11.

HARLAN, J. R. 1967. A wild wheat harvest in Turkey. *Archaeology*, vol. 20 (3), pp. 197–201.

HARLAN, J. R. & ZOHANY, D. 1966. Distribution of wild wheats and barley. *Science*, vol. 153, pp. 1074–1080.

HELBAEK, H. 1959. Domestication of food plants in the Old World. *Science*, vol. 130. pp. 365–372.

HELBAEK, H. 1966. Commentary on the phylogenesis of *Triticum* and *Hordeum*. *Economic Botany*, vol. 20, pp. 350–360.

HENSHALL, A. 1951. Textiles and Weaving Appliances in Prehistoric Britain. *Proc. Prehist. Soc.*, vol. 16 (1950), pp. 130–157 and Appendix A.

HIGGS, E. S. & JARMAN, M. R. 1969. The origins of agriculture: a reconsideration. *Antiquity*, vol. 43, pp. 31–40.

HOLE, F. 1962. Archaeological Survey and Excavation in Iran, 1961. *Science*, vol. 137, pp. 524–526.

HOLE, F. & FLANNERY, K. V. 1965. Early agriculture and animal husbandry in Deh Luran, Iran. *Current Anthropology*, vol. 6, pp. 105–106.

HOLE, F. & FLANNERY, K. V. 1967. The prehistory of southwestern Iran. *Proceedings of the Prehistoric Society*, vol. 33, pp. 147–204.

HOYLE, F. 1966. Speculations on Stonehenge. *Antiquity*, vol. 40, pp. 262–270.

HUTCHINSON, J. (Ed.) 1965. *Essays on crop plant evolution*. Cambridge.

IVERSEN, J. 1949. The Influence of Prehistoric Man on Vegetation. *Danmarks Geolog. Undersog.*, Copenhagen, IV, Bd. 3, no. 6, 27 pp., 3 pls.

IVERSEN, J. 1956. Forest Clearance in the Stone Age. *Scientific American*, 194, no. 3, pp. 36–41.

JORGENSEN, S. 1953. Forest Clearance with Flint Axes. *Fra Nationalmuseets Arbejdsmark*, 1953, pp. 109–110 (see also pp. 36–43).

KENYON, K. 1957. *Digging up Jericho*. 282 pp., 64 pls., 18 text-figs. London. (See also reports in *Palestine Exploration Quarterly* 1952–8.)

KIRKBRIDE, D. 1966. Beidha, an early Neolithic village in Jordan. *Archaeology*, vol. 19, pp. 199–207.

KIRKBRIDE, D. 1968. Beidha: early Neolithic village life south of the Dead Sea. *Antiquity*, vol. 42, pp. 263–274.

MACNEISH, R. S. 1965. The Origins of American Agriculture. *Antiquity*, vol. 39, pp. 87–93.

MANGELSDORF, P. C. 1965. The evolution of maize. In *Essays on Crop Plant Evolution* (ed. J. Hutchinson), Cambridge, pp. 23–49.

MELLAART, J. 1961. Excavations: Hacilar, *12th Annual Report British Institute of Archaeology at Ankara*, pp. 5–8.

MELLAART, J. 1962. Excavations at Çatal Hüyük. *Anatolian Studies*, vol. 12, pp. 41–65. 1963. *Anatolian Studies*, vol. 13, pp. 43–103. 1964. *Anatolian Studies*, vol. 14, pp. 39–119.

MELLAART, J. 1965. *Earliest Civilizations of the Near East*. 143 pp., 108 illus. London.

MOIR, J. R. 1939. *Grime's Graves, Weeting, Norfolk*. 24 pp., 3 text-figs. H.M. Stationary Office, London (Ancient Monuments, Official Guide).

MORTENSEN, P. 1964. Additional Remarks on the Chronology of Early Village-farming Communities. *Sumer*, vol. 20, pp. 28–36.

NANDRIS, J. 1968. Lepenski Vir. *Science Journal*, vol. 4, p. 64.

PERKINS, D. 1964. The Fauna from the Prehistoric Levels of Shanidar Cave and Zawi Chemi Shanidar. *INQUA Report of the VI International Congress on Quaternary, Warsaw 1961*. vol. II, pp. 565–571. Lodz.

PERROT, J. 1960. Excavations at Eynan ('Ein Mallaha). *Israel Exploration Journal*, vol. 10, pp. 14–22.

PIGGOTT, S. 1949. *British Prehistory*. 208 pp. London.

PIGGOTT, S. 1954. *The Neolithic Cultures of the British Isles*. xix+420 pp., 12 pls., 63 text-figs. Cambridge.

PIGGOTT, S. 1960. Neolithic and Bronze Age in East Europe. *Antiquity*, vol. 34, p. 285.

PITTIONI, R. 1956. Contributions to a Study of 'The Problem of Pile Dwellings'. *Proc. Prehist. Soc.*, vol. 21 (1955), pp. 102–107.

PROUDFOOT, B. 1961. The British Association's experimental earthwork. *New Scientist*, vol. 11, pp. 596–598.

QUENNELL, M. C. & H. B. 1955. *Everyday Life in the New Stone, Bronze and Early Iron Ages.* 5th ed., x+120 pp., 90 text-figs. London.

REED, C. A. 1959. Animal Domestication in the Prehistoric Near East. *Science*, vol. 130, pp. 1629–1638.

REED, C. A. 1961. Osteological evidence for prehistoric domestication in Southwestern Asia. *Zeitschrift für Tierzüchtung und Züchtungsbiologie*, vol. 76, pp. 31–38.

RENFREW, C. 1968. The domestication and exploitation of plants and animals. *Antiquity*, vol. 42, pp. 297–299.

RENFREW, C., DIXON, J. E. & CANN, J. R. 1966. Obsidian and Early Cultural Contact in the Near East. *Proceedings of the Prehistoric Society*, vol. 32, pp. 30–72.

RODDEN, R. J. 1962. Excavations at the Early Neolithic site at Nea Nikomedeia. Greek Macedonia (1961 season). *Proc. Prehistoric Society*, vol. 28, pp. 267–288.

RODDEN, R. J. 1964. A European Link with Çatal Hüyük: uncovering a 7th millennium Settlement in Macedonia. *Illustrated London News*, pp. 564–567; 604–607.

SAUER, C. O. 1952. Agricultural Origins and Dispersals. *Bowman Memorial Lectures, American Geographical Society.* v+110 pp., 4 pls. New York.

SOLECKI, R. S. 1963. Prehistory in Shanidar Valley, Northern Iraq. *Science*, vol. 139, pp. 179–193.

SREJOVIC, D. 1968. Lepenski Vir. *Illustrated London News*, Jan. 20, p. 23; Feb. 3, p. 27.

STAPLETON, H. E. 1953. Origin of Short-Horned Cattle. *Bull. Ann. Soc. Jérsiaise*, vol. 16, pt. 1, pp. 100–102.

STEARN, W. T. 1965. The Origin and Later Development of Cultivated Plants, (Masters Memorial Lecture, 1964). *Journal of the Royal Horticultural Society*, vol. 90, pp. 279–291.

STEENSBERG, A. 1943. Ancient Harvesting Implements. *Nat. Skrifter Ark.-Hist Raekke.*, Copenhagen, 1. 275 pp.

STONE, J. F. S. & WALLIS, F. S. 1952. Third Report of the Sub-Committee of the South-Western Group of Museums and Art Galleries on the Petrological Identification of Stone Axes, *Proc. Prehist. Soc.*, vol. 17 (1951), pp. 99–158.

UCKO, P. J. & DIMBLEBY, G. W. (Eds.) 1969. *The domestication and exploitation of plants and animals.* London. (In preparing this fifth edition, many authors in this valuable publication have been consulted, but to save space they have not been listed by name.)

VAN LOON, M. 1966. Mureybat: an early village in inland Syria. *Archaeology,* vol. 19, p. 215.

WATERBOLK, H. T. 1960. The 1959 carbon-14 symposium at Groningen. *Antiquity,* vol. 34, pp. 14–18.

WHITEHEAD, G. K. 1953. *The Ancient White Cattle of Britain and their Descendants.* 174 pp., 46 pls. London.

WISSLER, C. 1946. *The Cereals and Civilization.* 63 pp., 80 text-figs. American Mus. Nat. Hist., New York.

ZEUNER, F. E. 1954. Domestication of Animals. *In* C. Singer *et alia, A History of Technology,* Oxford, vol. 1, pp. 327–352.

ZEUNER, F. E. 1954. Cultivation of Plants. *Ibid.,* pp. 353–375.

ZEUNER, F. E. 1963. *A History of Domesticated Animals.* 560 pp. London.

Plates

Plate II

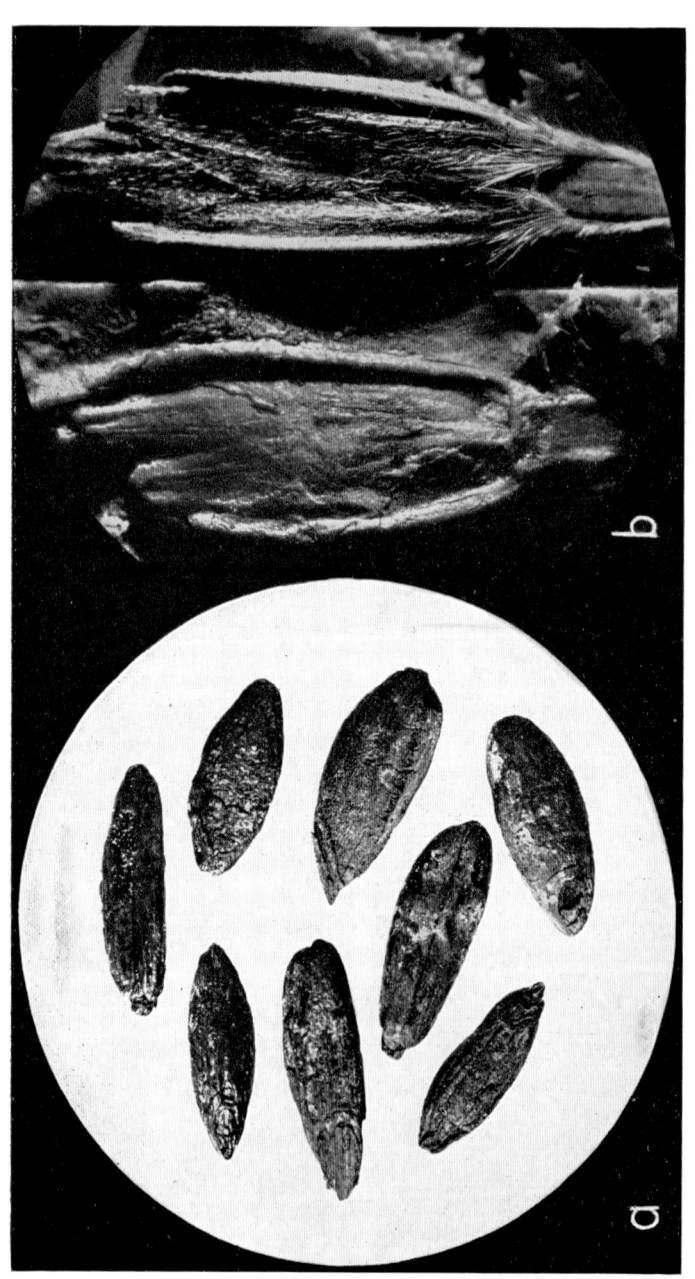

(a) Carbonized grains of wheat from pre-pottery Neolithic, Jarmo, Iraq (upper three einkorn, the remainder emmer); (b) Cast of Jarmo wheat spikelet (left) compared with recent emmer. Approx. ×5. *By courtesy of Dr. H. Helbaek and of the Oriental Institute, Chicago.*

Plate III

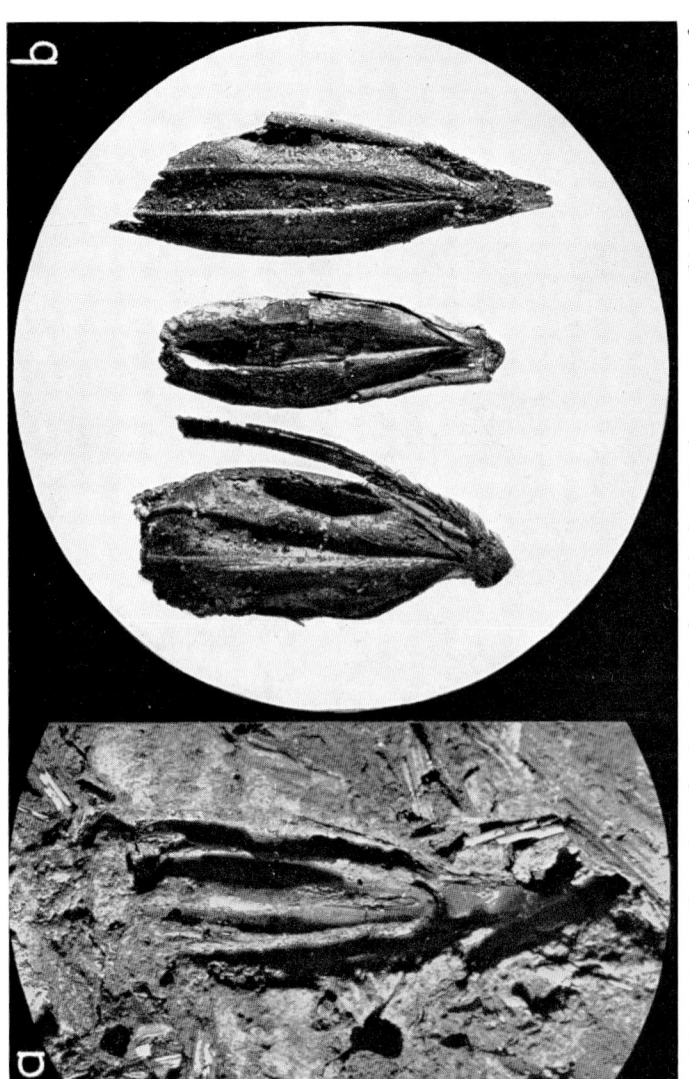

(a) Imprint in floor clay of spike-section of wild barley, *Hordeum spontaneum*; (b) Carbonized grains of sterile lateral florets of *H. spontaneum*. Pre-pottery Neolithic, Jarmo, Iraq. Approx. × 5. *By courtesy of Dr. H. Helbaek and of the Oriental Institute, Chicago.*

Plate IV

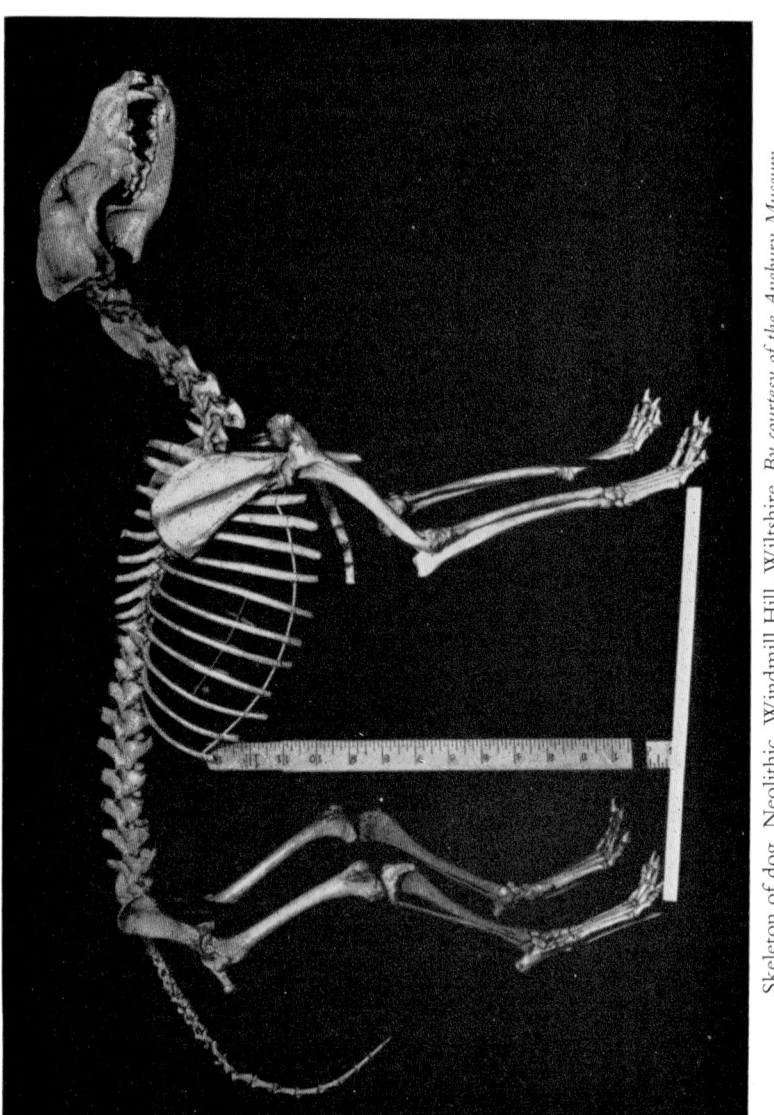

Skeleton of dog. Neolithic, Windmill Hill, Wiltshire. *By courtesy of the Avebury Museum.*

Plate V

Left: Bezoar goat, *Capra hircus aegagrus*, S.W. Asia. *After A. Brehm.* Right: Wild mouflon, *Ovis orientalis*, Cyprus. *Photo. by F. E. Zeuner.*

Plate VI

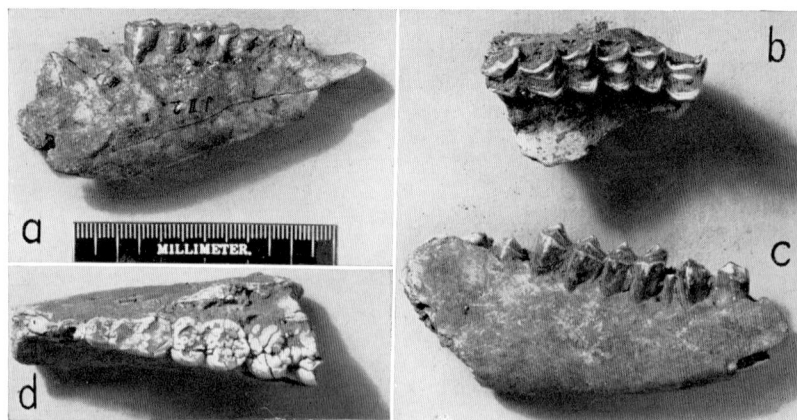

(a) Lower jaw fragment of goat; (b, c) lower and upper jaw fragments of sheep; (d) jaw fragment of pig. Pre-pottery Neolithic, Jarmo.

White park cattle of the Duke of Hamilton's herd at Cadzow, Lanarkshire. *After G. K. Whitehead.*

Plate VII

Wild sow with young, *Sus scrofa*.

Plate VIII

(a) Aurochs, *Bos primigenius*, from a sixteenth-century painting found in an antique shop in Augsburg in 1827. The last known specimen of the aurochs was killed in Poland in 1627. (b) 'Bred-back' aurochs believed to resemble the wild form very closely. This specimen was bred by Professor Heinz Heck, Director of the Tierpark, Hellabrun, München, in 1932.

After G. K. Whitehead: by courtesy of the Fauna Preservation Society.

Plate IX

Tree-felling in Denmark using a Neolithic polished stone axe-head. Three men cleared 600 square yards of birch forest in 4 hours and more than 100 trees were felled with the same axe-head, which had not been sharpened for about 4,000 years. *After Jorgensen.*

Plate X

A courtyard in Jericho, about 6,250 B.C. The woman is grinding corn in a quern and the flour falls into a limestone dish. The woman behind pours grain into a storage pit. *Drawing by Maurice Wilson.*

Plate XI

a

b

Baskets: (a) Boat-shaped basket made in coiled technique, possibly used in sowing corn. From grain-storage pit, Neolithic, Fayum. $\frac{1}{5}$. *After Caton-Thompson & Gardner*. (b) Miniature basket preserved in dry sand; Neolithic, Fayum. $\frac{3}{5}$. *By courtesy of University College, London.*

c

d

Leather containers: (c) from Early Dynastic grave, Nubia. *After Reisner*. $\frac{1}{10}$. (d) A reconstruction, in which the leather was drawn over a withy ring and sewn with strips of skin. $\frac{3}{10}$. Leather containers of similar type were probably made during Neolithic times and were evidently the prototypes for some kinds of pottery. *Reconstruction by John W. Waterer.*

Plate XII

(a) Limestone bowl, restored. ⅞. (b) Fragment of bowl in veined limestone, slightly enlarged. Pre-pottery Neolithic, Jarmo. *By courtesy of the Oriental Institute, Chicago.*

Plate XIII

a

b

(a) Bag-shaped pot reminiscent of a leather container. Neolithic, Windmill Hill, Wiltshire. $\frac{2}{5}$. *After A. Keiller*. (b) Pottery bowl (restored), Neolithic, Windmill Hill. $\frac{1}{2}$. *By courtesy of the Avebury Museum*.

Plate XIV

(a) Oldest example of a textile, perhaps woollen, adhering to a fragment of human thigh bone. Level VI, Çatal Hüyük, 6,500 B.C. *After J. Mellaart.* (b) Berber woman spinning. The spindle consists of a tapered stick weighted with a whorl. *Based on a photograph by D. D. Duncan; by courtesy of 'Life'.*

(c) Linen textile (reconstructed) from Neolithic lake-side village, Irgenhausen, Switzerland. About $\frac{1}{10}$. *Original in Landesmuseum, Zürich.*

Plate XV

Pottery figurines of the Neolithic Hamangia culture (c. 3,600 B.C.), Eastern Roumania. *After Berciu.*

Plate XVI

Neolithic town walls, Jericho, which was founded before 7,000 B.C. Five succes-sive town walls were built during the pre-pottery period. *After K. M. Kenyon.*

Plate XVII

a

Neolithic house foundations, Jarmo, Iraq. Houses of the pre-pottery period had built-in clay ovens (top centre) and clay basins baked into the floors (top right). *After R. J. Braidwood.*

b

'Boulder art' *in situ* at Lepenski Vir.
After D. Srejovic

Plate XVIII

Portrait heads of the pre-pottery Neolithic phase, Jericho. The features were modelled in plaster on actual skulls. The top of the lower skull is decorated with bands of black paint, perhaps representing a head-dress. *After K. M. Kenyon.*

Index